MW00882735

DAILY

DEVOTIONAL

for

WOMEN

365 DAYS OF 5-MINUTE
CHRISTIAN DEVOTIONS
FOR A LIFE OF LOVE, HAPPINESS,
AND INSPIRATION

**MADE
EASY
PRESS**

Producer & International Distributor
eBookPro Publishing
www.ebook-pro.com

DAILY DEVOTIONAL FOR WOMEN

365 Days of 5-Minute Christian Devotions
for a Life of Love, Happiness, and Inspiration

Made Easy Press

Copyright © 2024 Made Easy Press

All rights reserved. No parts of this book may be reproduced or
transmitted in any form or by any means, electronic or mechanical,
including photocopying, recording, taping, or by any information
retrieval system, without the permission, in writing, of the author.

Contact: agency@ebook-pro.com

ISBN

Introduction

Hi, my beautiful sister in Christ, and welcome to your year-long journey through faith.

By picking up this book, you've already taken the first step into a life of spirituality and goodness, and I congratulate you on your dedication!

Between these pages, you will find an endless trove of wisdom and encouragement, all drawn from unique and beautiful passages of the Bible, both the Old and New Testaments. Some of them will be familiar to you and some may be new, but each offers a small piece of God-given wisdom to brighten your day, fill you with hope, and bring you ever closer to His love.

All it takes is five minutes every day – whether you choose to devote your time first thing in the morning, during a break, or at the end of a long day, these cherished verses and their accompanying food for thought will fill the coming year with purpose.

I hope you enjoy reading these devotions as much as I enjoyed writing them.

Contents

January

1

"The righteous will live by faith."

Romans 1:17

As you begin your 365-day journey of commitment to your faith and yourself, take the time to reflect on what it truly means to "live by faith."

As Christians, we are encouraged to give our faith space in our everyday lives, and that is what makes us righteous and deserving of all the wonderful things God has in store for us.

With a brand-new year just beginning, how do you intend to live in faith this year?

2

"Do nothing out of selfish ambition or vain conceit. Rather, in humility value others above yourselves."

Philippians 2:3

New beginnings often mean new opportunities and with those come comparisons. It is a natural human tendency to compare our blessings, talents, and successes with those of the people around us, and we often find ourselves lacking.

But to have true humility is to accept that the success of others is in no way detrimental to your own. Why should we not celebrate the good in others' lives just as we celebrate the good in our own?

Dig deep to find that humility that will allow you to live a comparison-free, resentment-free life.

3

"For God did not send his Son into the world to condemn the world, but to save the world through him."

John 3:17

This verse encapsulates the heart of God's redemptive plan for humanity. Jesus Christ was not sent to earth to condemn us for our sins, but rather to offer us salvation and eternal life through His sacrifice on the cross. It's a powerful reminder of God's immense love and grace towards us, and the incredible gift of salvation that God offers freely to all who believe in His Son.

4

"Fear God and keep his commandments, for this is the duty of all mankind."

Ecclesiastes 12:13

The Bible urges us to "fear God and keep his commandments." But should we really fear Him, when He is the one who teaches us to love?

Fear of God is different from that which we ascribe to earthly things. When God tells us to fear Him, He means for us to have sufficient respect and reverence for a God who is mightier, more virtuous, and more knowing than we will ever be. When we "fear" God, we stay on a path of righteousness and grace. Not because we fear the consequences of our actions otherwise but because we understand that our heavenly father wants only what is best for us.

5

"Their sins and lawless acts I will remember no more."

Hebrews 10:17

Forgiveness is a virtue highly valued in Christianity. The ability to accept that someone has done wrong by you, and then to release those feelings of hurt and betrayal and finally allow peace into your heart is one that must be practiced and perfected.

True forgiveness can only come as soon as you understand that the actions of others are just that—their own. They do not reflect on you or your soul, nor are they your responsibility to bear. Once you accept that, you will find your heart to be softer and quicker to forgive.

6

"Consider it pure joy, my brothers and sisters, whenever you face trials of many kinds, because you know that the testing of your faith produces perseverance."

James 1:2-3

What trials do you face in life? And how do you view them? It is easy and natural to view trials as obstacles, to wish them gone, and to yearn for a challenge-free existence. But without challenges, where would we be? Mankind has grown, adapted, and persevered thanks in large part to being forced to innovate and overcome.

A life with no struggles would be a pointless one, indeed. James' wise words remind us that we can and must approach the trials of life with joy and enthusiasm, knowing that as our faith is tested and we persevere, we are only stronger.

7

*"My flesh and my heart may fail, but God is the
strength of my heart and my portion forever."*

Psalm 73:26

Our bodies are beautiful, wonderful things. They carry us through life and are a home for our souls, and they should be cherished and loved as a gift from God.

However, as amazing as it is, the body is a physical thing. It sometimes fails, and as we grow older it softens and weakens. We must take care to treat it with respect and nourish it well, but we must also remember that our true strength comes from God above.

He is the never-ending source of light and inspiration that lifts us up even when our bodies cannot.

8

*"Whatever you do, work at it with all your heart,
as working for the Lord, not for human masters."*

Colossians 3:23

Whether you're struggling with work, chores, studies, parenthood, or just balancing everything together, everything becomes easier when we see it not as something we are doing for anyone else—but as something we are doing for ourselves, and for the Lord.

When we allow our faith to guide our lives, that passion imbues our days and hours with a sense of true purpose, making it easier for us to give our all to every single task, be it big or small.

9

"The Lord will fight for you; you need only to be still."

Exodus 14:14

In the chaos of life's battles, we often find ourselves grasping for control, striving to overcome challenges through our own strength and efforts.

God assures us that he is our mighty defender, ready to fight on our behalf. He doesn't ask us to muster up our own army or devise elaborate strategies. Instead, He simply asks us to be still.

Being still doesn't mean being passive or resigned to defeat. Rather, it's an act of trust and surrender. It's about releasing our grip on worry and fear and entrusting our battles into God's capable hands.

10

"His divine power has given us everything we need for a godly life through our knowledge of him who called us by his own glory and goodness."

2 Peter 1:3

In this verse, we're reminded that God has already equipped us with everything necessary to live a life that reflects His character. Through our relationship with Him, we have access to His divine power, which enables us to navigate life with wisdom, grace, and godliness.

Today, let's lean into this truth, embracing the abundance of resources and strength that God provides. As you deepen your knowledge of Him, walk confidently in His calling, confident that He has prepared you for every step of the journey.

11

"Can a man walk on hot coals without
his feet being scorched?"

Proverbs 6:28

Proverbs paints a vivid image of the consequences of engaging in wrongful behavior. Just as walking on hot coals inevitably leads to burning, indulging in temptation leads to spiritual harm and a weakening of the soul.

The Bible reminds us of the importance of avoiding situations that can lead us astray. Instead, reflect on the choices you make and the company you keep. Take care to walk in righteousness, avoiding the snares of temptation and staying firmly grounded in your faith.

12

"Stop trusting in mere humans, who have but a breath
in their nostrils. Why hold them in esteem?"

Isaiah 2:22

This verse serves as a reminder of the limitations of human strength and wisdom. While people may seem powerful or influential, there are limitations to human strength and wisdom. Placing our trust solely in human beings will inevitably lead to disappointment.

But God Himself, who is an eternal and unchanging presence in our lives, is worthy of our trust and adoration. So when we choose to anchor ourselves in unwavering faithfulness, we can respect and indeed admire our deserving fellow humans while staying grounded in faith.

13

"Set a guard over my mouth, Lord;
keep watch over the door of my lips."

Psalm 141:3

The sin of gossip tempts us time and time again. Gossiping with a friend or sister can easily feel harmless—just a little chat between girls, a way to share what's been going on in your life.

But this psalm reminds us of an important thing. Every word that crosses our lips has tremendous power—power to lift people up and build up our world, or power to hurt, demean, and cause destruction.

So guard your mouth carefully and consider how you use your words—let every whisper between friends, family, and strangers bring nothing but good and light to the world.

14

"In the same way, count yourselves dead to sin
but alive to God in Christ Jesus."

Romans 6:11

This verse challenges us to embrace our identity in Christ. Through His death and resurrection, we have been set free from the power of sin and death. We are no longer slaves to our sinful nature but have been made alive in Christ. We have a choice—we can choose to align our thoughts and actions with this truth, or we can dismiss it. Let's live in the fullness of our new life in Christ, empowered by His Spirit to walk in righteousness and obedience. As we do, we'll experience the abundant life that Jesus came to give us.

15

*"For where you have envy and selfish ambition,
there you find disorder and every evil practice."*

James 3:16

When we allow jealousy and self-centeredness to take root in our hearts, as we often do without noticing, they inevitably lead to chaos and harmful behavior. Rather than encouraging unity and peace, they sow seeds of discord and division. Try to examine your heart and root out any traces of envy or selfish ambition. Instead, seek to uplift and encourage others, which will uplift you in turn. If everyone were to let go of jealousy, the world would be a far more loving, harmonious place.

16

*"So that your faith might not rest on human wisdom,
but on God's power."*

1 Corinthians 2:5

In a world filled with competing ideologies and philosophies, it's easy to rely on human wisdom to guide our faith. However, 1 Corinthians reminds us that true faith is grounded not in the wisdom of man, but in the power of the Almighty.

When we place our trust in God's strength, surrendering our dependence on human understanding, we open ourselves to experiencing His miraculous work in our lives.

The true magic is learning to combine our appreciation for human thought and progress with the certain knowledge that all knowledge lies with God above.

17

*"Be strong and courageous, for you will bring
the Israelites into the land I promised them on oath,
and I myself will be with you."*

Deuteronomy 31:23

In times of uncertainty and challenge, God's words to Joshua resonate deeply: "Be strong and courageous." Just as God assured Joshua of His presence and provision as he led the Israelites into the promised land, He promises to be with us on our own journeys.

He equips us with the strength and courage to face whatever lies ahead. With His presence guiding us, we can step forward boldly, knowing that He will fulfill His promises in our lives.

18

*"Teach us to number our days,
that we may gain a heart of wisdom."*

Psalm 90:12

This psalm invites us to reflect on the brevity and significance of our lives. By recognizing the finite nature of our days, we're reminded to live with intentionality and purpose. Each moment becomes precious, deserving of our careful consideration.

With this new insight, we can look at the small things in life and appreciate them far more; alternatively, we can recognize the *in*significance of things that may seem overwhelming and all-encompassing and realize that perhaps they are not so terrible after all.

19

*"You are altogether beautiful, my darling;
there is no flaw in you."*

Song of Solomon 4:7

In Song of Solomon, we witness an unwavering declaration of love and affirmation. Just as the beloved in the Song of Solomon is cherished and valued by her beloved, so too are we deeply loved and cherished by our Heavenly Father. Despite our imperfections and shortcomings, God sees us as beautiful and flawless. His love for us is unconditional and unwavering, and we too can and indeed should learn to notice the profound beauty in all people and things of God's creation.

20

*"I have hidden your word in my heart
that I might not sin against you."*

Psalm 119:11

This special verse hides a powerful and life-changing strategy for overcoming sin. By internalizing God's Word, we equip ourselves with the truth and guidance needed to resist temptation and live in alignment with His will.

The Word of God serves as a safeguard, offering wisdom and strength in moments of weakness. As long as we imbue our lives with Scripture and holiness, we can furnish our hearts and minds, providing them with a layer of protection against the temptation of wrongdoing.

January

21

"You are still worldly. For since there is jealousy and quarreling among you, are you not worldly? Are you not acting like mere humans?"

1 Corinthians 3:3

Paul addresses the Corinthians, urging them to examine their attitudes and behavior. He identifies jealousy and quarreling as evidence of a problematic mindset – one that is focused on selfish desires and earthly concerns rather than on God. We all sometimes allow worldly attitudes to influence our thoughts and actions. But real strength lies in training our hearts to seek unity, love, and humility in all our interactions.

22

"The Lord, the Lord, the compassionate and gracious God, slow to anger, abounding in love and faithfulness."

Exodus 34:6

God is described in the Book of Exodus as compassionate, gracious, slow to anger, and abounding in love and faithfulness. These attributes reveal the heart of our Heavenly Father – a God who is rich in mercy and steadfast in His love for us. However distant we may feel from Him, he is always, *always* waiting for us to return to Him. His love knows no bounds, and His faithfulness endures forever. We, too, should exemplify God by being steadfast in our relationships and generous with our affection.

23

"Taste and see that the Lord is good;
blessed is the one who takes refuge in him."

Psalm 34:8

Just as tasting food allows us to appreciate its flavor, experiencing God allows us to understand His goodness. The Psalm invites us to experience the goodness of the Lord fully. It's an invitation to encounter God personally, to cultivate a close and loving relationship with Him. When we take refuge in Him, we find ourselves surrounded by His love, protection, and provision. This helps us to overcome the challenges life sets before us with grace, knowing that God is there to support us.

24

"The Sovereign Lord is my strength; he makes my feet like
the feet of a deer, he enables me to tread on the heights."

Habakkuk 3:19

God equips us to face the challenges of life with confidence and perseverance. Just as he allows the deer to skillfully navigate rugged terrain with grace and agility, He strengthens us for the journey, enabling us to rise above our circumstances and conquer the highest peaks.

So place your trust in the Lord, knowing that He is your source of strength always and that with Him, you can overcome any obstacle.

25

*"In all my prayers for all of you,
I always pray with joy."*

Philippians 1:4

Here, we glimpse the heart of Paul's prayers for the believers – a heart filled with joy. Despite his circumstances, Paul's prayers overflowed with joy as he interceded for his brothers and sisters in Christ. This reveals the deep love and connection he shared with them, as well as his confidence in God's faithfulness. Paul's behavior and commitment to his people are and example to us all, to pray for others with joy. When you make prayer a part of your life, and pray for others as well as yourself, you become a partner of God in His work.

26

*"The prayer of a righteous person
is powerful and effective."*

James 5:16

Do you make prayer part of your daily routine? You can make it a custom to start the morning with prayer or give yourself a few minutes in the evening. However you incorporate it, prayers have incredible impact when offered by a person whom God deems as righteous.

The prayers of those who walk in righteousness are not only powerful but also effective, capable of bringing about transformation and breakthrough. As followers of Christ, we are so lucky to have been made righteous through His sacrifice, and our prayers carry weight and have the power to bring about real change.

27

*"In the beginning God created the
heavens and the earth."*

Genesis 1:1

These opening words of Scripture declare the foundational truth of God's existence and His creative power. Before anything else existed, God willed the universe into being. From the vast expanse of the heavens to the intricate details of the world we know, every element of creation reflects His wisdom and majesty.

We, too, should strive to live a life of creating. Devote your days to making the world a better place than it was, creating life, love, joy, and kindness in the small space you occupy in the universe.

28

*"You turned my wailing into dancing;
you removed my sackcloth and clothed me with joy."*

Psalm 30:11

Our faith and our relationship with God have such immense power in transforming our day-to-day. The simple knowledge that you are not alone, that there is a constant in your life that will never leave or forsake you, can turn every agony into joy and every challenge into triumph.

Remember that no matter how grim things seem or how hard it may be to get back up, God is always there waiting to clothe you with joy. It may take some time to come back to Him, to reconnect, but when you do, that joy will find you as it always does.

29

*"Start children off on the way they should go,
and even when they are old they will not turn from it."*

Proverbs 22:6

Whether you are a mother or not, whether you hope for children someday or are content without them, whether you are struggling with infertility or blessed with kids already, there is a lesson to learn from this special verse.

Whenever we interact with children, be they our own or not, we must keep in mind this important lesson. Young minds are so pliable and willing to learn. It is so important to set them on the right path and give them the tools they need to continue on it. Remember this, and you will be a blessing in the life of any child who is a part of yours.

30

*"But when you ask, you must believe and not doubt,
because the one who doubts is like a wave of the sea,
blown and tossed by the wind."*

James 1:6

Knowing when and how to question the things around you is an important part of life. We *should* encourage ourselves and others to ask questions, to be curious, and to seek answers of our own.

But when it comes to our faith, there is virtue in believing. Doubt will only undermine our faith, eroding our trust and flinging us into a sea of uncertainty. When you have faith, when you believe, you are fulfilled.

31

"Be strong, and let us fight bravely for our people and the cities of our God. The Lord will do what is good in his sight."

2 Samuel 10:12

S amuel urges the nation to "fight bravely for their people and the cities of our God."

We all have people we fight for—it can be our friends, family, partners, children, sometimes even strangers when we feel a cause is right. What, in your life, can represent the "cities of God"? What might your faith call you to fight for beyond the people whom you love?

Perhaps, as Christians, we are called to fight to spread the word and light of God. Perhaps we must fight to fill the world with good to outshine the bad. Give some thought to the things you fight for in life—is there anything more you could do?

February

1

"I will sing of the Lord's great love forever; with my mouth I will make your faithfulness known through all generations."

Psalm 89:1

As Christians, one of our obligations, and indeed our privileges, is to sing the Lord's praise loud for all to hear. Through easy and hard times, in our joyous moments and our greatest tragedies, through entire generations, we have a duty to make the love of God known to all the world.

You can do this by committing to your community and congregation, by being active in spreading the Word of God, or even by simply teaching your children and loved ones to love and cherish God in their lives as you do.

If you do this for Him, and certainly for the world, you will be worthy of every good thing He bestows upon you.

2

"Restrain your voice from weeping and your eyes from tears, for your work will be rewarded."

Jeremiah 31:16

Life hits us hard sometimes. No matter how faithful we are and how big a part of our life we make our Christianity, there is no escaping the challenges and difficulties of real life.

We all suffer and hurt from time to time, and it is natural and okay to allow those feelings to overcome you. True strength lies in the next moments—in being able to wipe your tears and get back up, believing that things will get better and that your pain and struggles will be rewarded in the end.

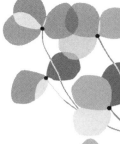

3

*"By myself I can do nothing; I judge only as I hear,
and my judgment is just, for I seek not to please myself
but him who sent me."*

John 5:30

"By myself, I can do nothing." Even the most powerful people in the world are still that—just people. When we forget this, we tend to believe that all we do is from ourselves and in our own power. But we know this to be false. As sound as our judgment may be, as great or small our accomplishments, we must remember that all we are and all we can become is thanks to Him, and the unending love He shows us.

4

*"For he has rescued us from the dominion of darkness
and brought us into the kingdom of the Son he loves,
in whom we have redemption, the forgiveness of sins."*

Colossians 1:13-14

You must never forget just what a service our Lord and Savior has done for you, in sacrificing himself for the redemption of your sins.

God, in his unfailing love and devotion to His Son, brought us into his kingdom and granted us an existence of light and joy. Appreciate this, and be grateful for it every day. Know that you are deserving, as are your fellow Christians, and use that knowledge to imbue every single day with meaning.

February

5

*"For it is by grace you have been saved, through faith—
and this is not from yourselves, it is the gift of God."*

Ephesians 2:8

This verse encapsulates the essence of the gospel message: our salvation is a gift from God, received by faith through His grace. We cannot earn or merit salvation through our own efforts alone; it is solely by God's unmerited favor that we are saved. This truth humbles us and fills us with gratitude for the incredible love and generosity of our Heavenly Father. It is our duty to respond with faith and thanksgiving, living each day in the light of His grace and sharing the good news of salvation with others.

6

*"Be careful not to practice your righteousness
in front of others to be seen by them. If you do,
you will have no reward from your Father in heaven."*

Matthew 6:1

The Bible, in Matthew 6, teaches us a useful lesson in humility. Many of us may think that righteousness is something to flaunt, to show the world, and to set an example with, for others. But here, we learn that the opposite is true.

God wants nothing more from you than true, honest righteousness. He does not wish you to advertise your good deeds, rather He appreciates you so much more when you are good, kind, and just and expect nothing in return. Being able to be truly fulfilled inside just by knowing you are doing right by the world is the greatest level of righteousness you can reach.

7

"Do not say, 'Why were the old days better than these?'
For it is not wise to ask such questions."

Ecclesiastes 7:10

Our life is split into three: the past, the present, and the future. What's past is past—over and done. We can learn from it, certainly, and look back fondly on memories we cherish. But when we let ourselves wallow completely in the past, grieving for what was, we miss out on so much of the present, and we risk our future.

Just like we drive with our eyes straight ahead, looking out for what is to come, so should we spend our life in hope and expectation for all the things that yet await.

8

"The unfolding of your words gives light;
it gives understanding to the simple."

Psalm 119:130

This Psalm beautifully illustrates the transformative power of God's Word. When we immerse ourselves in Scripture, studying it daily, its truth unfolds before us, illuminating our path and bringing clarity to our minds. Even the simplest among us can gain wisdom and understanding through the teachings of God's Word. Be sure to always approach the Scriptures with an open heart and a teachable spirit, allowing God to shed His light upon you and lead you into a deeper relationship with Him.

February

9

"I sought the Lord, and he answered me;
he delivered me from all my fears."

Psalm 34:4

When we turn to the Lord in prayer and earnest seeking, He responds with His comforting presence and mighty deliverance. Our fears may be numerous and overwhelming, but in God's presence, they lose their power. As we seek Him, He replaces our fears with His peace and assurance.

Whatever fears may be weighing us down, we can bring them to God in prayer, trusting in His faithfulness to deliver us. In His presence, we will find refuge and strength to face any challenge with confidence and courage.

10

"Mercy, peace and love be yours in abundance."

Jude 1:2

Jude bestows upon us a powerful blessing, overflowing with divine grace and goodness. Mercy, peace, and love are extended to us in abundance through the richness of God's character. His mercy offers forgiveness and redemption, His peace brings calm in the midst of life's storms, and His love envelops us with unconditional acceptance and care. And frankly, what more can we ask for if we have these three blessings? In God's abundant provision, we find strength, comfort, and joy for the journey ahead.

11

"Those who are wise will shine like the brightness
of the heavens, and those who lead many to righteousness,
like the stars for ever and ever."

Daniel 12:3

Wisdom and leadership are two values highlighted in this beautiful metaphor from the Book of Daniel. We are urged to be wise and shine like the heavens, and to be leaders of others to righteousness.

Wisdom and leadership don't always go together—they require such different skill sets.

But there is beauty in learning to combine the humility and intelligence of wisdom with the confidence and determination of leadership. And when you do, as you can, you will be a person who is looked up to and admired by her surroundings, as well as appreciated and beloved by God.

12

"You are to be holy to me because I, the Lord, am holy,
and I have set you apart from the nations to be my own."

Leviticus 20:26

God makes sure in Leviticus 20 to point out just how special His people are to him. He has imbued every single one of us with just a little of His own holiness, which makes us one with Him and one with our people.

Cherish that uniqueness in you, foster it carefully, and channel it into thoughts and actions that are deserving of the piece of God that resides within you.

February

13

*"And a voice came from heaven: 'You are my Son,
whom I love; with you I am well pleased.'"*

Mark 1:11

In this moment of Jesus' baptism, we are privy to a profound declaration from heaven affirming Jesus' identity as the one beloved Son of God. This divine pronouncement echoes through generations, revealing the deep love and approval of the Father for His Son. It serves as a reminder of the intimate relationship between the Father and the Son, and as beloved children of God, we, too, receive assurance from this promise of unwavering affection.

14

*"One who has unreliable friends soon comes to ruin,
but there is a friend who sticks closer than a brother."*

Proverbs 18:24

Friends are the family you choose. If you've ever had a true friend who has stuck with you through the hardest times and encouraged and supported you to be your best self, you know that these words ring true.

The Bible reminds us of the importance of friends who are as close as family—sometimes even closer. Take stock of your relationships and see which ones are precious to you. Cherish these and invest effort into maintaining them. Learn also to let go of those relationships that do more harm than good.

15

*"Listen to your father, who gave you life,
and do not despise your mother when she is old."*

Proverbs 23:22

O ur parents or caregivers have played a significant role in our lives, giving us life and nurturing us from infancy to adulthood. As they grow older, though our relationship with them may change, they continue to deserve our love, care, and attention. This verse is a call to honor our parents with our words, actions, and attitudes, recognizing the wisdom and experience they possess.

16

*"Be strong and courageous, and do the work.
Do not be afraid or discouraged,
for the Lord God, my God, is with you.
He will not fail you or forsake you until all the work for
the service of the temple of the Lord is finished."*

1 Chronicles 28:20

A s David prepares to build the temple of the Lord, he charges his son Solomon with this order. It's a powerful reminder that God's presence and provision accompany us in every task He calls us to undertake. Like Solomon, we're encouraged to be strong, courageous, and diligent in the work set before us, knowing that God is with us every step of the way. His faithfulness ensures that we will never be overcome by fear or discouragement.

February

17

*"My help comes from the Lord,
the Maker of heaven and earth."*

Psalm 121:2

In times of trouble or uncertainty, it's natural and important to seek assistance and guidance from friends, family, and professional counsel. Yet, as believers, we're reminded in this verse that our ultimate help comes from the Lord Himself. He is not only our Creator but also our Sustainer and Provider. When we turn to Him in prayer, we're tapping into the boundless resources of the One who made heaven and earth. Whatever challenges we may face, He is more than able to meet our needs and guide us through every situation.

18

*"For the Spirit God gave us does not make us timid,
but gives us power, love, and self-discipline."*

2 Timothy 1:7

The devout followers of Christ are not called to live in fear or timidity. Instead, the Spirit fills us with power, love, and self-discipline, enabling us to live boldly and victoriously. His power equips us to overcome obstacles, His love urges us to help others selflessly, and His self-discipline helps us to reach the highest peaks of success. With His empowering presence, we can face any challenge with confidence and courage.

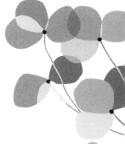

19

"Dear friend, do not imitate what is evil but what is good.
Anyone who does what is good is from God.
Anyone who does what is evil has not seen God."

3 John 1:11

John calls on us to emulate goodness and righteousness, avoiding the ways of evil. Those who choose to do what is good demonstrate their alignment with God and His will. Conversely, those who engage in evil reveal their separation from God and His truth. We Christian women should strive to live lives filled with goodness and righteousness, reflecting the light of God's love and truth to the world around us.

20

"Be sure to fear the Lord and serve him faithfully with all
your heart; consider what great things he has done for you."

1 Samuel 12:24

Fearing the Lord doesn't mean being afraid of Him, but rather revering Him and acknowledging His sovereignty and majesty. When we serve God faithfully with all our heart, we honor Him and express our gratitude for His countless blessings and the great things He has done for us.

As we reflect on His blessings, may our hearts be stirred to serve Him with renewed dedication and passion, bringing glory to His name in all that we do.

February

21

"Satisfy us in the morning with your unfailing love,
that we may sing for joy and be glad all our days."

Psalm 90:14

Just like breakfast is the most important meal of the day, mornings are a perfect time to devote to prayer and reflection.

This Psalm reflects a beautiful prayer for God's unfailing love to fill us each morning, bringing satisfaction and joy that lasts long into the evening, giving us strength as we go about our daily business of work, chores, errands, meals, and family time. When we choose to start our day by seeking God's love and presence, we invite Him to satisfy the deepest longings of our hearts and fill us with His peace and joy.

22

"Therefore what God has joined together,
let no one separate."

Mark 10:9

Here, Jesus affirms the sanctity and permanence of marriage. God's design for marriage is a sacred union, joining two people together as one. It's a relationship built on love, trust, and commitment, and showing that love for all to see. As followers of Christ, we're called to honor and uphold the institution of marriage, recognizing it as a steady constant in our lifetime.

Whether you are married, hoping to marry, or single, focus your heart on cultivating a safe, strong relationship with a significant other that will last you a lifetime.

23

*"These commandments that I give you today are to
be on your hearts. Impress them on your children.
Talk about them when you sit at home and when you walk
along the road, when you lie down and when you get up."*

Deuteronomy 6:6-7

As we have been taught since we were kids, the commandments of God are not just rules to follow, but principles to live by — they are to be deeply ingrained in our hearts and minds. As mothers, sisters, aunts, godmothers, teachers, and mentors, we have a responsibility to teach and model these truths to the children in our lives. Whether at home, on the go, or at rest, try to seize every opportunity to share God's word and His ways with the younger generation. Through intentional teaching and living out our faith, we can leave a lasting legacy of faithfulness and obedience to God's commandments.

24

*"The Lord is good, a refuge in times of trouble.
He cares for those who trust in him."*

Nahum 1:7

In this verse from the Old Testament, we can find reassurance in the goodness and faithfulness of the Lord. He is not only good but also a reliable refuge for us in times of trouble, always there to provide shelter and strength through life's struggles. He cares deeply for those who trust in Him, providing comfort, guidance, and protection.

February

25

"But love your enemies, do good to them, and lend to them without expecting to get anything back."

Luke 6:35

This may be one of the most difficult things we are commanded to do in the Bible. Jesus challenges us to embody a radical form of love that transcends our natural inclinations. Loving our enemies, doing good by them, and lending without expecting repayment are acts that go against human nature but reflect the true heart of God.

As followers of Christ, we're called to imitate His selfless love, extending kindness and generosity to all, regardless of how they may respond. Take a moment to think about your enemies—who are they? How have they hurt you? And how can you find it in your heart to treat them with grace and kindness, nonetheless?

26

"Consequently, faith comes from hearing the message, and the message is heard through the word about Christ."

Romans 10:17

Faith is not a product of our own efforts or intellect but is a response to the proclamation of the gospel. As we hear and engage with the messages of Christ, our hearts are stirred, and our faith is awakened. It is through the hearing of God's Word that we come to understand His love, His grace, and His plan of salvation for us. That is why it is so important to prioritize hearing and meditating on the Word of God, allowing it to strengthen and deepen our faith in Christ.

27

*"Therefore, as God's chosen people, holy and dearly loved,
clothe yourselves with compassion, kindness,
humility, gentleness and patience."*

Colossians 3:12

The Bible reminds us of our identity as God's chosen and beloved children. Just as we choose clothing to cover and adorn ourselves, we are told to intentionally "clothe" ourselves with qualities that mirror Christ's compassion, kindness, humility, gentleness, and patience. These virtues not only honor God but also bless those around us and allow our lives to become a testimony to the transformative power of God's love at work within us.

28

*"When Jesus landed and saw a large crowd, he had
compassion on them, because they were like sheep without
a shepherd. So he began teaching them many things."*

Mark 6:34

Despite His own weariness, Jesus's compassion moved Him to minister to the people, recognizing their spiritual hunger and their longing for guidance. His response teaches us the importance of compassionately reaching out to those who are lost and in need of direction. Just as Jesus taught and cared for the crowd, we are called to extend compassion to those around us, offering hope and guidance through the teaching of God's Word.

March

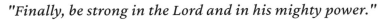

1

"Finally, be strong in the Lord and in his mighty power."

Ephesians 6:10

In this verse, Paul urges believers to draw their strength not from their own abilities or resources, but from the Lord and His power. As we face the challenges and struggles of life, it's easy to rely on our own strength, but the true source of strength lies in God alone. When we lean on Him, we tap into His infinite power, which is more than sufficient to sustain us through every trial and temptation.

2

"Therefore, since we are surrounded by such a great cloud of witnesses, let us throw off everything that hinders and the sin that so easily entangles. And let us run with perseverance the race marked out for us."

Hebrews 12:1-2

These beautiful verses encourage us to embrace the journey of faith with determination and perseverance. The "great cloud of witnesses" refers to the faithful men and women who have gone before us, testifying to the power of God's grace and the victory of faith. Their lives serve as examples for us, inspiring us to cast aside anything that hinders our spiritual growth and to run with endurance the race of real life before us. Like athletes training for a race, we too must fix our eyes on Jesus and train every day to be closer to Him.

3

"I can do all this through him who gives me strength."

Philippians 4:13

In a powerful declaration, Paul acknowledges his dependence on Christ for strength and ability. We are limited in our own abilities, but with Him, we are empowered to overcome any challenge or obstacle.

Whatever you encounter, whether it's hardship, temptation, or uncertainty, you can confidently declare, "I can do all this through him who gives me strength." Let that be a mantra for you in times of struggle.

4

"And we boast in the hope of the glory of God.
Not only so, but we also glory in our sufferings,
because we know that suffering produces perseverance;
perseverance, character; and character, hope."

Romans 5:2-4

Suffering, though difficult, produces perseverance – a steadfastness that enables us to endure trials with unwavering faith. Instead of shrinking away from suffering, we are called to embrace it, knowing that through it, God works to refine and strengthen us.

As we persevere, our character is molded, and we become more like Christ, marked by virtues such as patience, resilience, and compassion. Ultimately, this journey of suffering and perseverance leads to hope – a confident expectation of God's promises and His faithfulness to fulfill them.

March

5

*"Ascribe to the Lord the glory due his name;
bring an offering and come before him. Worship the
Lord in the splendor of his holiness."*

1 Chronicles 16:29

Worshipping God is not merely an act of singing songs or saying prayers; it's an expression of the heart that acknowledges His supremacy above all else. Ascribing glory to His name involves acknowledging His sovereignty, majesty, and worthiness of praise. When we bring our offerings and come before Him, we are presenting our lives as living sacrifices, holy and pleasing to Him. And when we worship Him fully, He repays us with love, compassion, and kindness.

6

*"Therefore, my dear brothers and sisters, stand firm.
Let nothing move you. Always give yourselves fully to the
work of the Lord, because you know that your
labor in the Lord is not in vain."*

1 Corinthians 15:58

Giving ourselves fully to the work of the Lord involves dedicating our time, talents, and resources. It's a labor of love that may require sacrifice and perseverance, but we can be confident that our efforts are not in vain. Every act of service, every word spoken in His name, and every seed of faith sown will bear fruit in due time. Despite the challenges and trials we may face, we are called to stand firm, anchored in the truth of God's Word and the promises of His faithfulness.

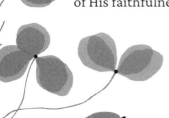

7

"But the fruit of the Spirit is love, joy, peace, forbearance, kindness, goodness, faithfulness, gentleness and self-control."

Galatians 5:22-23

The Bible lists the characteristics that manifest in the lives of those who are filled with the Holy Spirit. Just as a tree bears fruit, so too do believers exhibit these qualities as evidence of their relationship with God. As we allow Him to work in our hearts and lives, we begin to reflect the love, joy, peace, and other virtues that characterize God's nature.

8

"But for you who revere my name, the sun of righteousness will rise with healing in its rays."

Malachi 4:2

The "sun of righteousness" in this verse symbolizes the coming of God's righteousness and the light of His presence, which brings healing and wholeness to our lives and the lives of those around us. By revering and honoring His name, we open ourselves to receive the healing and restoration that only He can bring—like a sun rising in the morning to begin a fresh new day.

March

9

"For if you forgive other people when they sin against you, your heavenly Father will also forgive you."

Matthew 6:14

Forgiveness is a central aspect of the Christian faith, reflecting God's grace and mercy towards us. When we extend forgiveness to those who have wronged us, even in the worst way, we mirror the forgiveness we have received from our heavenly Father. Just as God freely forgives us of our sins, He calls us to forgive others in turn. It's not always easy to forgive, especially when we've been deeply hurt, but grudges are a prison or resentment from which forgiveness releases us to breathe freely again.

10

"In the beginning was the Word, and the Word was with God, and the Word was God."

John 1:1

In the deeply profound opening verse of the Gospel of John, we're introduced to the concept of the "Word." This "Word" is none other than Jesus Christ, the Son of God, who took on human form to dwell among us. Just as words convey thoughts, ideas, and messages, Jesus Christ is the expression of God's love, wisdom, and truth to humanity. He is the living Word who reveals God's character and purposes to us.

11

*"May he give you the desire of your heart
and make all your plans succeed."*

Psalm 20:4

Our Heavenly Father is our greatest supporter. He looks on at us like his children, wishing for us to follow the right path and cheering for us when we do. He wants what we want for ourselves, and He supports our plans, so long as they align with His purpose for our life.

When we find that purpose, and align our choices to it, no one is happier to give us the desire of our hearts than our one loving God.

12

*"We have this hope as an anchor for the soul,
firm and secure."*

Hebrews 6:19

Hope is described here as an anchor for the soul—firm and secure. Just as an anchor keeps a ship steady amidst rough waters, our faith in God's promises provides stability in life's storms. This hope isn't wishful thinking; it's a confident assurance in God's faithfulness. When life feels uncertain, you know that you can anchor your soul in this hope, finding strength and peace knowing that God is with you, steadying you through every challenge.

13

*"Because of the Lord's great love we are not consumed,
for his compassions never fail."*

Lamentations 3:22

Despite the challenges and trials we face, God's love surrounds us, preventing us from being overwhelmed. His compassion is unwavering, never running dry or faltering. No matter how difficult our circumstances may seem, God's love and compassion remain constant. They are our anchor in the storms of life, offering hope and reassurance that we will not be consumed by our struggles. When you struggle, stumble, or fall, look to God for His love which lifts us up time and time again.

14

*"Do not turn me over to the desire of my foes,
for false witnesses rise up against me,
spouting malicious accusations."*

Psalm 27:12

In Psalm 27:12, the psalmist pleads with God for protection against the schemes of his enemies. It's a cry born out of desperation, as he faces the threat of false accusations and malicious intent. Yet, amidst the turmoil, the psalmist places his trust in God's faithfulness and righteous judgment. This verse reminds us that in times of adversity, we can turn to God for refuge and deliverance. He sees the truth behind the deceitful words of our adversaries and will ultimately vindicate the innocent. So, we can entrust our troubles to God, knowing that He is our defender and refuge in times of trouble.

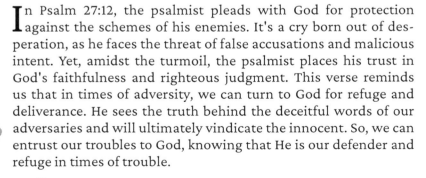

15

*"Like a snow-cooled drink at harvest time is
a trustworthy messenger to the one who sends him;
he refreshes the spirit of his master."*

Proverbs 25:13

Just as a refreshing drink cools and invigorates the weary farmer during harvest time, so can a faithful messenger rejuvenate the spirit of their master. When we prove ourselves to be trustworthy and faithful in our words and actions, we not only bring refreshment to others and ourselves but also honor God. Our relationships and responsibilities are imbued with integrity and dependence, leading to a more fulfilling existence.

16

*"Make it your ambition to lead a quiet life: You should
mind your own business and work with your hands, just as
we told you, so that your daily life may win the respect of
outsiders and so that you will not be dependent on anybody."*

1 Thessalonians 4:11-12

The Bible encourages us to strive for a quiet life of hard, honest work. By leading a quiet life, focusing on our own responsibilities, and working diligently with our hands, we not only earn the respect of those around us but also avoid unnecessary dependence on others. This approach fosters a sense of dignity and integrity in our daily lives. Moreover, it reflects our commitment to being responsible keepers of the gifts and opportunities that God has given us.

March

17

"She speaks with wisdom, and faithful instruction is on her tongue."

Proverbs 31:26

The holy Scripture has many wonderful and empowering things to say about women, and this might be one of the most powerful. A woman who is wise and faithful is held in esteem over every other. She is modest and humble, and she instructs others faithfully without expecting anything in return. Every word she says is intentional and she imparts true wisdom when she speaks. To be such a woman is a blessing, and for your loved ones to have you in their life is far more than they could ever wish for.

18

"Call to me and I will answer you and tell you great and unsearchable things you do not know."

Jeremiah 33:3

Have you ever called to God? We often think of calling out to God as a desperate last resort in times of woe. But your life will change when you realize that you can call to Him at any time, for anything. God has infinite capacity to bestow His love and affection upon you, all you have to do is ask for it.

An entire world of "great and unsearchable things" is out there, waiting for you to connect and discover. So why wait? Make it a habit to speak with God and seek His wisdom and guidance on all matters.

19

*"For the Lord your God is he who goes with you to fight
for you against your enemies, to give you the victory."*

Deuteronomy 20:4

This verse speaks to God's faithfulness and His commitment to His people. It encourages us to trust in His power and presence, knowing that He is always with us in every battle we face. It reminds us that we are not alone in our struggles; the Lord our God goes with us and fights on our behalf. He is our ultimate defender and champion, ensuring victory over our enemies.

Your "enemies" may be actual people who wish you evil, or something more abstract—like insecurities, mental health struggles, or an overwhelming lifestyle. No matter which enemy you are facing, God is on your side, rooting for you and helping you through.

20

*"Now, our God, we give you thanks,
and praise your glorious name."*

1 Chronicles 29:13

In our often fast-paced lives, it's essential to cultivate a spirit of gratitude and praise, making time and freeing mental space for acknowledging God's faithfulness and sovereignty. When we pause to give thanks to God and lift up His glorious name, we shift our focus from our own somewhat insignificant, though important, circumstances to something far bigger than us.

This sense of gratitude can and should be applied to the people around us as well—we should be constantly focusing on our blessings and our appreciation of them.

March

21

"Do not be afraid. I bring you good news that will cause great joy for all the people. Today in the town of David a Savior has been born to you; he is the Messiah, the Lord."

Luke 2:10–11

The good news shared in this verse is no less than that of the birth of the Messiah, our Lord and Savior. It brings with it a message of hope, joy, and salvation for all people. It's a reminder that God's plan for redemption is not limited to a select few but extends to every person, regardless of background or circumstance. The birth of Jesus in Bethlehem signifies the fulfillment of God's promise to send a Savior who would bring light into the darkness and peace to a troubled world—just as He promises always to redeem us from our troubles.

22

"How great you are, Sovereign Lord!
There is no one like you, and there is no God but you,
as we have heard with our own ears."

2 Samuel 7:22

This powerful proclamation by King David resonates with us today, reminding us of the unmatched majesty and power of our God. He is sovereign over all creation, ruling with wisdom, grace, and love. None can compare to His glory or match His infinite attributes.

In return, we respond with worship and adoration. We acknowledge His greatness and surrender to His authority, knowing that we are privileged to serve Him.

23

"Until now you have asked nothing in my name.
Ask, and you will receive, that your joy may be full."

John 16:24

One of the hardest things for women is often to ask for things for ourselves. We are so preoccupied with making sure others have all they need, and caring for our families and loved ones, that we sometimes forget to care for ourselves.

But we are deserving of joy and good things, we need only ask. God begrudges us nothing, He wants us to be happy always. Ask, and you will receive.

24

"As the body without the spirit is dead,
so faith without deeds is dead."

James 2:26

True faith is not merely intellectual assent or passive belief; it is dynamic and transformative, manifesting in tangible acts of love, obedience, and service. Our faith is demonstrated and validated by the way we live our lives and how we treat others.

Just as a body without a spirit is lifeless, so too is faith without corresponding actions.

We should strive to cultivate a living faith—one that is evidenced by our actions and attitudes. Let's seek opportunities to put our faith into practice, serving others with humility, compassion, and grace.

March

25

"Declare his glory among the nations,
his marvelous deeds among all peoples."

1 Chronicles 16:24

There are countless ways for us devoted Christian women to declare God's glory. Even if we don't have a million-follower social media presence or hold a position of power within our community, the power we have to spread the truth of God's Word is immense.

We can glorify His name through our actions, our words, our lifestyles. When we choose to live a life of faith and we are vocal about how proud we are to be His children, we are doing our part in return for all the good He has blessed us with.

26

"The Lord God said, 'It is not good for man to be alone.
I will make a helper suitable for him.'"

Genesis 2:18

We have all felt the bite of loneliness at a time in our lives. Humans need connection, touch, partnership, to feel fulfilled in their lives. Even God saw this as soon as He had created man—and gave him a woman for a companion.

It is incredibly important to work on yourself as an individual, to feel fulfilled and happy in your own skin. But do not forget that it is God's will for you to find a committed and loving partnership, as well.

27

"Be strong and very courageous. Be careful to obey all the law my servant Moses gave you; do not turn from it to the right or to the left, that you may be successful wherever you go."

Joshua 1:7

God and his disciples have given us all the tools we need to live a good, righteous life. All we must do is follow the laws and commandments we have been given, committing to a routine of faithfulness and walking in His path.

This success that the Bible speaks of is success in everything—in our personal relationships, our professional endeavors, and our own self-development. Living God's Word will put us on the right path for better things in all areas of our lives.

28

"I praise you because I am fearfully and wonderfully made; your works are wonderful, I know that full well."

Psalm 139:14

It is not always easy to appreciate just how wonderfully made we are. Just how much thought, detail, and love has been poured into every single essence of our being, from the smallest molecules of our body to the intangible things that make us who we are.

But never forget that everything we are is proof and the result of God's wonderful works and His absolute devotion to us, His beloved children.

March

29

"Return to me, and I will return to you."

Malachi 3:7

Our relationship with God is all about mutuality. When life takes us further from our faith at times, we lose that connection we have with our Heavenly Father. And when it steers us back, it comes back in full force, just where we left off.

Just like with any relationship, we need to work at it. We need to make time for just us, put thought, effort, and intentionality into our actions, and make it a priority.

When we do, God reciprocates in kind, and we are welcomed into His arms as though we had never left them.

30

"See, the Lord your God has given you the land. Go up and take possession of it as the Lord, the God of your fathers, told you. Do not be afraid; do not be discouraged."

Deuteronomy 1:21

In this passage, God commands the Israelites to take possession of the land He has promised them. Despite the challenges and uncertainties they may face, He urges them not to be afraid or discouraged, for He is with them.

When God calls us to a task, He equips us with everything we need to fulfill His plans. Let's not allow fear or discouragement to hold us back from stepping into the fullness of what God has in store for us. Instead, let's walk in faith, seizing His promises with confidence, knowing that He is faithful to fulfill them.

31

*"Be strong and courageous. Do not be afraid;
do not be discouraged, for the Lord your God
will be with you wherever you go."*

Joshua 1:9

As Joshua prepared to lead the Israelites into the Promised Land, he faced daunting uncertainties. Yet, God reassured him that He would be with him every step of the way.

Similarly, in our own lives, we may face uncertainties about the future, obstacles on our paths, or fears that threaten to hold us back. In those moments, God's word to Joshua resonates with us.

We are reminded not to be afraid or discouraged, for the Lord goes before us and accompanies us wherever we go. With God by our side, we can face any challenge, overcome any obstacle, and press forward in faith.

April

1

"The grace of the Lord Jesus Christ
be with your spirit."

Philemon 1:25

We speak often about grace, but what does it truly mean? Grace is one of the defining virtues of our Lord and Savior, Jesus Christ. Grace encompasses so many things—it is the power to forgive those who have wronged us, it is benevolence, and favor toward others, it is the humility to forego your own needs and wants for those of a greater good.

When we behave with grace in our lives, we channel the virtues of Christ, basking in His example and shining His light upon the world.

2

"Let the little children come to me, and do not hinder them,
for the kingdom of God belongs to such as these."

Mark 10:14

Children possess a beautiful simplicity in their faith—they believe without doubting, love without reservation, and trust without question. Jesus encourages us to embrace this childlike faith, unencumbered by the pride, skepticism, or cynicism that is often present in adults.

Consider how you approach Him in your life; do you come to Him with open-heartedness and the trust of a child? Or are you reserved, plagued by doubt? Try to shed those obstacles, remembering what it was like to look upon God with the pure awe of a child.

3

"Love the Lord your God with all your heart and with all your soul and with all your mind and with all your strength."

Mark 12:30

To love God with all our heart means to offer Him our deepest affections and desires. It's about prioritizing Him above all else and finding our greatest joy and fulfillment in His presence.

Loving God with all our souls involves surrendering our innermost being to Him—our emotions, will, and spiritual essence.

To love God with all our minds requires engaging our intellect and understanding in seeking Him. It's a call to study His Word, meditate on His truths, and grow in knowledge and wisdom.

4

"When he spoke to me, I was strengthened."

Daniel 10:19

When Daniel received a visitation from an angelic messenger, he experienced a remarkable strengthening of his spirit.

Just as Daniel found strength when the angel spoke to him, we too can find renewed courage and fortitude in our encounters with God. It is as simple as spending time in prayer, meditating on His Word, or experiencing His presence in worship.

Know that in His presence, you can find the courage, resilience, and inner fortitude you need to face every challenge.

April

5

"To him who is able to keep you from stumbling and to present you before his glorious presence without fault and with great joy—to the only God our Savior be glory, majesty, power and authority, through Jesus Christ our Lord, before all ages, now and forevermore!"

Jude 1:24-25

This verse speaks to the power and faithfulness of our God. It reassures us that no matter what challenges we face, He is capable of upholding us and guiding us through every trial. He is our ever-present help in times of need, our rock and our refuge.

As we entrust ourselves into His capable hands, He promises to lead us into His glorious presence, where we will stand blameless and filled with joy.

6

"With him is only the arm of flesh, but with us is the Lord our God to help us and to fight our battles."

2 Chronicles 32:8

No matter what obstacles human beings have faced, there has never been great and complete victory without God's divine intervention. Often, we may find ourselves relying on our own abilities or resources to face the challenges before us. We can do much and are strong, intelligent, and resilient, but we will never be as powerful as we are when God is fighting on our side.

7

*"But go and learn what this means:
I desire mercy, not sacrifice."*

Matthew 9:13

As followers of Christ, it's easy to get caught up in performing religious duties or adhering to strict rules. However, Jesus reminds us that what truly matters to God is not that we forego our happiness or peace in sacrificing everything for Him.

Instead, he asks that we condition our hearts and our willingness to extend mercy and grace to those around us. That is the true essence of being a faithful Christian.

8

*"Blessed are the peacemakers,
for they will be called children of God."*

Matthew 5:9

In a world filled with strife and discord, the call to be peacemakers is more relevant than ever. This means seeking to mend broken relationships, fostering understanding amidst differences, and promoting unity and equality in our communities.

Being a peacemaker requires humility, patience, and a willingness to bridge divides. It involves listening with empathy, speaking with gentleness, and extending forgiveness even in the face of hostility. When we actively engage in the work of reconciliation, we reflect the character of our heavenly Father, who is the ultimate source of peace.

9

"Every good and perfect gift is from above,
coming down from the Father of the heavenly lights,
who does not change like shifting shadows."

James 1:17

Take a minute to reflect on your abundant blessings. What are you thankful for?

These gifts we are granted—family, health, wellbeing, money, a place to live, friends, occupation, intelligence—these are all from above. Certainly, we are deserving and worthy of them, but they are not of our own doing.

It is a comfort, then, to know that they do not depend on the fickle decisions of our human mind, but are consistent and constant like our Heavenly Father.

10

"Those who consider themselves religious and yet
do not keep a tight rein on their tongues deceive
themselves, and their religion is worthless."

James 1:26

This scathing but powerful message addresses the importance of controlling our tongues. It's easy to speak without considering the impact our words have on others, but James reminds us that true religion involves more than mere worship.

Our words have the power to build up or tear down, to encourage or discourage, to heal or wound. When we fail to control our tongues, we diminish the effectiveness of our faith. Our religion becomes hollow and meaningless if our speech doesn't align with the principles exemplified by Christ.

11

"Where then are the gods you made for yourselves?
Let them come if they can save you when you are in trouble!
For you, Judah, have as many gods as you have towns."

Jeremiah 2:28

Throughout history, nations have battled with the question of God. Can there truly be just one almighty God? Many ancient cultures turned to idols in search of an answer to the question of divine providence.

Today, idols may take many forms in our lives—material possessions, achievements, relationships, or even ideologies. But when trouble comes, these false gods prove powerless to save us. They offer no true comfort or refuge.

God alone is worthy of our worship and trust. He alone can truly save us.

12

*"Everyone who does evil hates the light, and will not
come into the light for fear that their deeds will be exposed.
But whoever lives by the truth comes into the light,
so that it may be seen plainly that what they have done
has been done in the sight of God."*

John 3:20-21

Those who choose to live in darkness, indulging in evil deeds, instinctively avoid the light for fear of exposure. Yet, those who embrace truth willingly step into the light, allowing their actions to be readily seen.

Whenever we know we are acting in a way that is unkind, selfish, or wrong, we tend to hide our actions from others. This should be a clear sign to us to stop and think—and correct our path. When we walk in light, we have nothing to hide.

13

*"God's voice thunders in marvelous ways;
he does great things beyond our understanding."*

Job 37:5

Job was a man who knew countless struggles. The Lord tested him time and time again, and yet, even among the trials and tribulations he faced, he knew one eternal truth: God does great things beyond our understanding.

To accept and truly know this is to glimpse the grandeur of the Lord. Though we may struggle to grasp the full extent of His works, let us humble ourselves before Him and draw closer to Him every day.

14

"In all these things we are more than conquerors through him who loved us."

Romans 8:37

Paul lists a series of terrible things that might befall a person in life. Then, he adds this inspiring verse, showing that no hardship is so terrible that it could stop Christ from loving us, or take away our love of Christ. Through the power of Christ's love, we are not only able to conquer any obstacle, but indeed we are more than conquerors. We have God's eternal love, which lifts us up to new heights of victory.

15

"From the Lord comes deliverance. May your blessing be on your people."

Psalm 3:8

When we face challenges, whether they are physical, emotional, or spiritual, we can turn to the Lord in prayer, seeking His guidance and intervention. He is our ever-present help in times of need, and His blessings abound for those who trust in Him. When we place our faith in the Lord and rely on His love and mercy, we can rest assured that He will deliver us from every trial and shower us with blessings.

April

16

"I am the good shepherd. The good shepherd
lays down his life for the sheep."

John 10:11

The image of a shepherd laying down his life for his sheep portrays the selflessness and unwavering commitment that Jesus has toward us. Just as a shepherd will do anything to protect his flock from harm, Jesus willingly endured suffering and ultimately gave His life on the cross to save us from sin and eternal separation from God.

We are not only God's children, we are His flock—and He will protect us from harm.

17

"And over all these virtues put on love,
which binds them all together in perfect unity."

Colossians 3:14

When we practice love in our interactions with others and with ourselves, it transforms our attitudes, actions, and relationships. Love compels us to show kindness, patience, forgiveness, and compassion towards one another.

Love transcends differences, heals divisions, and brings people together, and it is the healing power that can mend discord, hurt, and pain.

18

*"If my people, who are called by my name, will humble
themselves and pray and seek my face and turn
from their wicked ways, then I will hear from heaven,
and I will forgive their sin and will heal their land."*

2 Chronicles 7:14

God has offered us a profound promise. He assures us that if we
are humble, pray, seek His face, and turn from our wicked ways, He
will respond to our pleas.

Repentance plays a pivotal role in this process. Turning away
from sinful ways will demonstrate our sincerity and desire for
transformation. God promises to respond to such humility, prayer,
and repentance with forgiveness, healing, and restoration.

19

*"I know, my God, that you test the heart
and are pleased with integrity."*

1 Chronicles 29:17

Above all, integrity is appreciated by our Father. It encompasses
honesty, moral uprightness, and consistency in one's actions,
regardless of circumstances. Integrity stems from the very core
of our being. It means living a life of honesty, even when no one
else is watching. God sees beyond the surface and examines the
motives and intentions of our hearts. When our hearts are tested,
and our integrity shines through, it pleases God because it reflects
a genuine commitment to righteousness.

April

20

"God may yet relent and with compassion turn from his fierce anger so that we will not perish."

Jonah 3:9

In the Book of Jonah, the people of Nineveh embark on a journey of self-improvement and atonement, acknowledging that God is not only just and righteous but also compassionate and merciful. Despite their past transgressions and the imminent threat of judgment, they hold onto hope that God may relent from His fierce anger.

We can learn from their example that it is never too late to humble ourselves, acknowledging our need for God's mercy. No transgression is serious enough that He will not allow us to return to Him.

21

"Greater love has no one than this: to lay down one's life for one's friends."

John 15:13

Friendship is a powerful force, at times even stronger than the ties of blood. A good friend who is with you through thick and thin is more valuable than anything else and deserves our equal devotion to them.

The Bible tells us that the very highest level of goodness, of love, is sacrificing your own wants and needs for those of such a friend. Next time you meet with a friend or speak with one on the phone, make sure you are mindful of putting their needs and desires first—giving them your full and undivided attention.

22

"Surely the Sovereign Lord does nothing without revealing his plan to his servants the prophets."

Amos 3:7

God does not act arbitrarily or impulsively but instead operates with purpose and intentionality, often disclosing His intentions through His chosen messengers, the prophets.

God's willingness to communicate His plans demonstrates His desire for His people to be informed and aligned with His purposes. Through the prophets, God provides insight into His will, warnings of impending judgment, and promises of redemption and restoration. He invites His people to participate in His divine work by responding obediently to His revealed word.

23

"As the Father has loved me, so have I loved you. Now remain in my love. If you keep my commands, you will remain in my love, just as I have kept my Father's commands and remain in his love."

John 15:9-10

Jesus blesses us with an unfailing love that mimics the very same love He and His Father share. Just think what an incredible blessing it is for us to be rewarded with such a deep and steady commitment when all we are asked to do is to keep His commandments.

As long as we stay on the path of virtue, that love is ours in plenty and abundance. We can remain in His love from the day we are born until the day we die if so we choose to do.

April

24

"Stand up in the presence of the aged, show respect for the elderly and revere your God. I am the Lord."

Leviticus 19:32

In this important passage, God commands His people to show respect and honor to the elderly. This directive carries profound significance, emphasizing the invaluable merit of wisdom, experience, and the dignity of every individual, regardless of their age.

Respecting the elderly is more than a courtesy; it's a reflection of our reverence for God Himself. When we honor the aged, we acknowledge the wisdom accumulated over their years of living and recognize the image of God reflected in every person, regardless of their years on Earth.

25

"Cast all your anxiety on him because he cares for you."

1 Peter 5:7

It is natural at times to feel overwhelmed and anxious when things aren't going smoothly. We encounter troubles at work, problems with money, illness, and other stress-causing factors.

Luckily, we have in God an extra back willing to help us shoulder our burdens. When we entrust our worries to God, we acknowledge His sovereignty and our dependence on Him. We recognize that He is not only capable of carrying our burdens but also willing to do so out of His boundless love for us.

26

*"I am the Lord; that is my name! I will not yield
my glory to another or my praise to idols."*

Isaiah 42:8

In a world filled with distractions and competing voices vying for our attention and devotion, Isaiah 42:8 serves as a powerful declaration of our God's divine sovereignty and exclusivity.

He is not merely one among many deities to be worshipped; He is the Almighty, the Creator of heaven and earth, and there is no other besides Him.

As believers, we are called to honor and worship God alone, recognizing His unmatched greatness and majesty. We are invited into a relationship with the Creator of the universe, who desires our love and devotion above all else.

27

*"No branch can bear fruit by itself; it must remain in the
vine. Neither can you bear fruit unless you remain in me."*

John 15:4

In the beautiful analogy of the vine and branches, Jesus illustrates a truth about our relationship with Him. Just as branches draw their sustenance and vitality from the vine, so too do we find our strength, purpose, and fruitfulness in Jesus Christ. Without Him, we are powerless to produce lasting fruit in our lives. We may strive and toil, but true growth and abundance come only through our connection to Him.

April

28

*"So God created mankind in his own image,
in the image of God he created them;
male and female he created them."*

Genesis 1:27

In the beginning, when God created the Earth, sun, stars, seas, skies, plants, and animals, He set human beings apart from all His other creations.

No other animal or plant was created in His holy image—only us, mankind, males and females alike.

We are privileged and humbled to be God's chosen children in every way, carrying his very essence in our image. We must do all we can to justify this choice and to make Him proud of our every thought and action.

29

*"The Lord is gracious and compassionate,
slow to anger and rich in love."*

Psalm 145:8

God's grace and compassion know no limits. He extends His mercy to us even when we least deserve it, patiently waiting for us to turn to Him in repentance and faith. His love for His children is rich and unending, and He is slow to anger, even when we fail Him.

We ourselves should learn from these virtues and curb our anger, choosing instead to be patient and compassionate. We should give our love freely and without reserve, just as we are loved by the Almighty.

30

"In him we have redemption through his blood,
the forgiveness of sins, in accordance with
the riches of God's grace."

Ephesians 1:7

The price of our redemption as a people did not come cheap. It required the sacrifice of God's only Son, who gave His life on the cross for our sins. Through His death and resurrection, we were redeemed in God and offered the gift of eternal life.

Let us not take our redemption lightly. It is a precious gift, freely given but purchased at great cost. Let us live mindfully every day, devoting our days with intention to do good in this world.

May

1

*"For no one can lay any foundation other than
the one already laid, which is Jesus Christ."*

1 Corinthians 3:11

The world offers various foundations upon which people build their lives—wealth, success, relationships, and power, to name a few. However, none of these foundations can provide lasting security or eternal significance.

Only Jesus Christ, unchanging and steadfast, offers a foundation that endures through every storm and trial. When we build our lives upon the foundation of Jesus Christ, we find forgiveness for our sins, strength for our weaknesses, and hope for our future.

2

*"Do not rebuke an older man harshly,
but exhort him as if he were your father."*

1 Timothy 5:1

Respect for elders is a value deeply rooted in many cultures and societies, and it finds its roots in the biblical principle of honoring one another. As Christians, we are called to treat older individuals with kindness, gentleness, and deference, just as we would our own fathers.

This does not mean that we should refrain from offering correction or guidance when necessary. Rather, it means approaching such situations with humility, sensitivity, and love. Instead of rebuking harshly, we are encouraged to recognize the wisdom and perspective that often come with age.

3

"The name of the Lord is a fortified tower;
the righteous run to it and are safe."

Proverbs 18:10

In times of trouble and uncertainty, where do you find refuge? When we run to the Lord's name, we find shelter from the storms of life. His arms are a place of strength, where we can find courage in the face of fear, peace in the midst of chaos, and hope in times of despair. It is a place where we are reminded of His faithfulness, His promises, and His unending love for us.

Run to the Lord with confidence, knowing that He is a present help in trouble.

4

"Now faith is confidence in what we hope for
and assurance about what we do not see."

Hebrews 11:1

Faith is often described as believing in something that cannot be seen. It can be challenging to hold onto faith when we are so accustomed to seeking and expecting proof. Yet, Hebrews 11:1 tells us that faith is both "confidence in what we hope for and assurance about what we do not see."

Our faith is anchored in the promises of God and the truth of His Word. We may not always see immediate results or have all the answers to our questions right away, but we know that God is working behind the scenes, even when we cannot see it with our physical eyes.

May

5

"Therefore we do not lose heart.
Though outwardly we are wasting away,
yet inwardly we are being renewed day by day."

2 Corinthians 4:16

Not one of us is exempt from the hardships of life. Throughout our years, we encounter physical ailments, emotional turmoil, or spiritual battles that threaten to overwhelm us and topple the balance we so carefully construct in life.

However, while our outward circumstances may seem to deteriorate, our inner being is constantly being revitalized by the power of God. Even when our bodies weaken and suffer, our inner being is being strengthened and renewed all the time by the presence of Christ.

6

"Your word is a lamp for my feet,
a light on my path."

Psalm 119:105

The incredible power of God's Word lies in its ability to light our path and shine the way. You need only immerse yourself in the Scripture to discover a fantastic, inspiring world of God-given guidelines better and more meaningful than any self-help book ever written by man or woman.

The true art of Christian faith is learning how to apply God's Word to your life in the way it was meant, to truly live each day guided by His teachings and advice.

7

"Now may the Lord of peace himself give you peace at all times in every way. The Lord be with all of you."

2 Thessalonians 3:16

Peace is an elusive state. We pray often for peace, perhaps not really understanding how true peace is achieved.

Peace is not circumstantial. It does not depend on what is happening to or around you at the moment, on global events or happenings in your own little corner of the world. Peace is a state of mind. It comes when we are really and truly comfortable with ourselves and our place in this world. We can have peace at all times and in every way, with God's loving help.

8

"The mind governed by the flesh is death, but the mind governed by the Spirit is life and peace."

Romans 8:6

Our mind and body are two separate, yet strongly connected parts of us. Our mind is where we think, feel, imagine, and believe, and it needs guidance, and a helping hand to steer it through life.

We can choose to allow our body to govern our minds—to be led by our basic human wants and needs. But that is no life. Instead, let us allow the Holy Spirit to drive our thoughts and emotions, imbuing us with life and peace.

May

9

*"Be joyful in hope, patient in affliction,
faithful in prayer."*

Romans 12:12

There is a time and a place for everything.

In Romans 12:12, the Bible urges us to use our emotions wisely. When we are hopeful for something, it encourages us to take joy in that hope, in knowing that good things lie ahead. To live in the moment, not always waiting for what is to come.

When things are hard, it emboldens us to have the presence of mind to know that this, too, shall pass.

And when we pray, the Bible tells us to put our entire faith into that simple act, instilling our words and wishes with loyal faithfulness.

10

*"Therefore do not worry about tomorrow,
for tomorrow will worry about itself.
Each day has enough trouble of its own."*

Matthew 6:34

We live in the present, whether we wish to or not. The past is gone, and we may look back on it with fondness or regret. The future is unknown—and holds its own challenges and joys.

Trying to live our life in the past or the future is an exercise in futility. Live in the now, bask in this wonderful state of being, and curb your worries over what lies ahead. What will come will come, for good or bad, whether you spend your days worrying about it or not.

11

"God is love. Whoever lives in love lives in God, and God in them."

1 John 4:16

When 1 John 4:16 states that, "God is love," what does that mean? God is almighty, He is our Father, our shepherd, how can he be "Love"?

The Scripture goes on to explain that "whoever lives in love; lives in God."

When we choose to live our lives led by the value of love, doing our best to love everyone and everything that crosses our path, we are privileged to live in the very essence of God. And in the same way, when we achieve this, we allow God a place of warmth and acceptance within us, where He can dwell.

12

"Do not withhold good from those to whom it is due, when it is in your power to act."

Proverbs 3:27

We've all been tasked at some time or another with the challenging choice between doing good when we know we can or choosing instead to focus on ourselves.

But Proverbs encourages, even commands us, to never refrain from being good to those who deserve it. Even when we are tired, have better things to do, or simply feel like acting a little selfishly, we should remember these words. Just as we want and expect the Lord to show us kindness and good when they are our due, so should we, His messengers on Earth, be good when it is in our power to be so.

May

13

"I consider everything a loss because of the surpassing worth of knowing Christ Jesus my Lord, for whose sake I have lost all things."

Philippians 3:8

We tend to measure success by the accumulation of worldly possessions, achievements, and recognition. However, Paul's words challenge this perspective, highlighting the worth of knowing Christ Jesus our Lord. For Paul, knowing Jesus was not merely about intellectual knowledge but about an intimate relationship that transformed his entire being.

May we, like Paul, prioritize cultivating a deep, intimate relationship with Him above all else.

14

"The Lord is my strength and my song; he has become my salvation."

Exodus 15:2

When we feel weak, we can find strength in the Lord. As we lean on Him, He infuses us with the strength we need to press on.

Then, the Lord becomes our song of praise and gratitude. When we reflect on His goodness and unfailing love, our hearts overflow with adoration. He is the reason for our joy, and His salvation brings a melody of hope and renewal to our souls.

15

"Blessed is the one who trusts in the Lord,
whose confidence is in him."

Jeremiah 17:7

Faith is believing even though you have no empirical or physical proof. It is a notion reserved especially for the divine, for the other-worldly. But trust is something we know from our lives. We trust our parents to raise us, our teachers to educate us, our bosses and managers to respect us, and our friends to have our back. Trust means being sure that someone will come through for us, no matter what.

This is the kind of trust we can put in our Lord. We can trust Him to be by on our side for He will never fail us. And when we place our trust and confidence in Him, we are blessed.

16

"I have loved you with an everlasting love;
I have drawn you with unfailing kindness."

Jeremiah 31:3

In this declaration, our Heavenly Father promises that His love and affection for His children are everlasting. He has loved us since the very first day and will continue to love and bless us with unwavering kindness.

He drew us in, took us under His wing to be His chosen and beloved people, and He will never go back on His promise to love us for eternity.

May

17

"In him was life, and that life was the light of all mankind. The light shines in the darkness, and the darkness has not overcome it."

John 1:4-5

John refers to Jesus in this verse as "The Light," a glowing beacon that shines in the darkness and can never be extinguished. The Lord is made of life, and that life is bestowed upon every living being, in the form of light.

Light is knowledge, awareness, understanding, and exposure. It is the essence of being intentional in your actions and thoughts, in saying, "I do not hide." He gives us light, which is ours to live in, should we choose to.

18

"Love is patient, love is kind. It does not envy, it does not boast, it is not proud."

1 Corinthians 13:4

The thing about true, lasting, devoted love, is that it is pure. You can have love for a partner, a family member, a friend, a pet, a co-worker, or even a stranger. How can you know if your love is true? When you read this verse, and think to yourself, "That sounds just like the love I have for X," you can know that that love is real.

When you truly love someone you are not jealous. You are patient with them and slow to anger. You do not feel the need to boast about your connection, but you feel it deep inside, where it really matters.

19

*"Wisdom is a shelter as money is a shelter,
but the advantage of knowledge is this: that wisdom
preserves the life of its possessor."*

Ecclesiastes 7:12

This important verse makes a comparison and distinction between two coveted resources; money, and knowledge. Similarly, both of these are things that people work hard to acquire. We need both money and wisdom to live, but the important thing to remember is that the worth of money does not exceed beyond its earthly value. Money is our means of succeeding in our mortal life. Wisdom, on the other hand, has the immense power to literally preserve your life, opening your mind to God and allowing you to be in His favor, in this life and the next.

20

"Let the one who boasts boast in the Lord."

1 Corinthians 1:31

Boasting our riches and blessings before others is an act that is undesirable to God. God appreciates modesty and values humility above all else, preferring us to refrain from loudly advertising what we have in order to make others feel worse about their own circumstances.

Instead, if you wish to boast about anything, take pride in your loving and loyal connection with the Lord. Shout out to the world just how great He is, and sing His praise to all who wish to hear.

21

"Rejoice always."

1 Thessalonians 5:16

This seemingly simple commandment is perhaps one of the most challenging to fulfill. How can we possibly rejoice always? We face struggles, hardships, and obstacles, and while there are certainly good and even wonderful times, not every minute is one that we find it easy to rejoice in.

And yet, there is strength and even courage in finding something to rejoice in, no matter what your circumstances. Every rain cloud has a silver lining, every storm has its blessings. When we learn to find joy in every single aspect of life, good or bad, we fulfill God's greatest wish for us—to rejoice always.

22

"If we confess our sins, he is faithful and just and will forgive us our sins and purify us from all unrighteousness."

1 John 1:9

The act of confession is central to Christianity. We learn from a young age that it is okay to make mistakes, to stray from the path of good. But when we do stumble, the only way to fix things and return to the path of light is to clear your heart and conscience of what you have done. Unconfessed sins will sit and fester, weighing on our soul and hindering our spiritual growth.

When we confess our sins, even if only by acknowledging them to ourselves and to God, He forgives us, purifies us, and leads us back to our faith.

23

"Rise up; this matter is in your hands.
We will support you, so take courage and do it."

Ezra 10:4

Responsibility and accountability are things that we learn as we grow up. When we enter adulthood, we begin to understand the weight of being responsible for ourselves and, later, our families.

Accountability is crucial to our independence. We must be aware that our life is in our hands, and our actions have consequences. Ezra 10:4 reminds us of this—this matter is in our hands. But, in the same breath, we are reassured that though we must look after ourselves, we will always have the support of our Heavenly Father.

24

"Though your sins are like scarlet,
they shall be as white as snow; though they are
red as crimson, they shall be like wool.'"

Isaiah 1:18

It is important to remember that though we sin, our sins do not have to stain our souls forever. Every person has the benefit of having his or her sins erased, forgotten, and their soul cleansed and pure once again.

Everyone sins, because everyone is human. We must not allow our falls to bring us down, rather we must rise up, brush ourselves off, and learn and improve in order to do better next time.

25

*"Six days do your work, but on the seventh day do not work,
so that your ox and your donkey may rest, and so that
the slave born in your household and the foreigner
living among you may be refreshed."*

Exodus 23:12

Rest is not a privilege—it is a necessity. What with work, family, and the manifold obligations we face, it is so easy to allow ourselves to burn out without notice. But God cares for us and reminds us to rest. Even our animals and those who are not of our household deserve rest, recuperation, and a chance to start fresh. Let's make sure to find some time each day to wind down and find that peace that will allow us to keep going strong.

26

*"And let us consider how we may spur one another on
toward love and good deeds, not giving up meeting together,
as some are in the habit of doing, but encouraging one
another—and all the more as you see the Day approaching."*

Hebrews 10:24-25

Christianity is all about community and togetherness. When we gather together as a community of believers, we strengthen and uplift one another, providing support and encouragement to all. This fellowship is not merely a social gathering but a vital component of our spiritual growth and perseverance. So do not neglect community, or the opportunity to share in your faith with others, be it at Church or anywhere else.

27

"In Christ and through faith in him we may approach God with freedom and confidence."

Ephesians 3:12

Before Christ, humanity stood separated from God by sin and its consequences. But through Christ's sacrifice, the abyss that once separated us from God was closed, granting us unrestricted access to our Father. As believers, we no longer need to fear or hesitate to approach God; instead, we can boldly come into His presence, knowing that we are welcomed with open arms.

Approaching God with freedom and confidence doesn't mean we come arrogantly or flippantly. It means we come humbly, yet assured of His love and acceptance. We can pour out our hearts before Him, knowing that He hears our prayers and cares deeply for us.

28

"Everyone who calls on the name of the Lord will be saved."

Romans 10:13

The beauty of this verse lies in its simplicity and inclusivity. It doesn't demand any specific prerequisites; rather, it extends an open invitation to all who recognize their need for a Savior. It speaks to the heart of every individual, regardless of background, status, or past mistakes.

No matter who you are, what you have done, or how strong your faith has been before when you call on the name of the Lord in true, devoted surrender, He will be your Savior.

May

29

"Restore us to yourself, Lord, that we may return;
renew our days as of old."

Lamentations 5:21

We sometimes wake up to find ourselves in seasons of spiritual low or distance from God. Distractions can lead us away from the vibrant faith we once knew. Yet, like the people of Israel, we always have the opportunity to turn to the Lord and seek His restoration.

And when we do so, when we understand what we are missing and yearn to return to His arms, He will renew our connection as if it had never been lost.

30

"If someone slaps you on one cheek, turn to them the
other also. If someone takes your coat,
do not withhold your shirt from them.
Give to everyone who asks you, and if anyone takes
what belongs to you, do not demand it back.
Do to others as you would have them do to you."

Luke 6:29-31

Turning the other cheek and giving freely to those in need may seem impractical or even foolish in the eyes of the world. However, Christianity teaches us that true strength lies in humility and love, not in seeking revenge or holding onto material possessions.

By following Jesus' example of selfless love, we demonstrate His transformative power in our lives. When we extend grace and forgiveness to others, we bring healing and restoration to broken relationships and communities.

31

"Do not be yoked together with unbelievers.
For what do righteousness and wickedness have in common?
Or what fellowship can light have with darkness?"

2 Corinthians 6:14

Paul's instruction here is not about avoiding interaction with unbelievers altogether but rather about being cautious about the depth of our partnerships and associations. He highlights the fundamental differences between righteousness and wickedness, light and darkness, emphasizing that these opposing forces cannot coexist harmoniously.

We have the duty and the privilege to surround ourselves with people who encourage us in our faith journey, challenge us to grow spiritually, and hold us accountable to God's standards.

June

1

"As far as the east is from the west, so far has he removed our transgressions from us."

Psalm 103:12

The vivid imagery of God removing our sins "as far as the East is from the West" portrays the vastness of His grace and the completeness of His pardon. When we come to God in repentance, seeking His forgiveness, He doesn't merely overlook our transgressions or sweep them temporarily under the rug. Instead, He chooses to cast them away from us completely, separating them from us in an irreversible manner. In turn, we are expected to extend the same kindness and forgiveness to those around us.

2

"Do everything in love."

1 Corinthians 16:14

In just four simple words, 1 Corinthians 16:14 encapsulates a profound commandment that lies at the heart of the Christian faith: "Do everything in love."

Love is not merely an emotion or a fleeting feeling; it is a choice, a deliberate action that we are called to exercise in every aspect of our lives. Whether in our interactions with family, friends, neighbors, or even strangers, love should infuse our words, our actions, and our attitudes.

Ultimately, the greatest demonstration of love is found in the example of Jesus Christ, who laid down His life for us out of love. His sacrificial love serves as the ultimate model for us to follow as we seek to love God and love others.

3

"After they prayed, the place where they were meeting was shaken. And they were all filled with the Holy Spirit and spoke the word of God boldly."

Acts 4:31

In our journey of faith, we are called to lean on the Holy Spirit for strength and courage in sharing the gospel message. Just as the early disciples experienced a tangible manifestation of the Spirit's presence, we can also seek His guidance and empowerment through prayer and careful attention.

As we open our hearts to the work of the Holy Spirit, He empowers us to be effective witnesses for Christ in our communities, workplaces, and spheres of influence. Thus, we can face any challenge with confidence, knowing that His power is at work within us.

4

"With this in mind, we constantly pray for you, that our God may make you worthy of his calling."

2 Thessalonians 1:11

In 2 Thessalonians 1:11, Paul expresses his heartfelt desire to see his fellow believers grow in their faith and walk worthy of the calling they have received from God. He is not praying for himself but for the good of others.

Naturally, when we pray, we focus on us. What are we thankful for, what do we wish for, where is our head at? But when we pray for others, demonstrating our concern for them and inviting God's work into their lives, we achieve an even higher level of spiritual growth and inspiration than ever before.

5

"If you do not obey the Lord, and if you rebel against his commands, his hand will be against you, as it was against your fathers."

1 Samuel 12:15

Throughout the Bible, we see the pattern of blessings for obedience and discipline for disobedience. Our God is a kind and generous Father, but He also holds us accountable for the consequences of our actions. Just like a parent educating a child, sometimes He needs to show us discipline to invite and encourage us to repent, reconcile, and return to His waiting arms.

6

"Be strong and courageous. Do not be afraid or terrified because of them, for the Lord your God goes with you; he will never leave you nor forsake you."

Deuteronomy 31:6

As God prepares to help Joshua lead the Israelites into the Promised Land, He urges him to "be strong and courageous." Fear has a way of paralyzing us, of making us doubt our abilities and the safety of our future. But God's presence dispels fear. It reminds us that we are not alone, that we have a faithful and mighty God who is for us and never against us.

So, whatever you're facing today, take courage. You are not walking this journey alone. Be strong and courageous, knowing He is with you always.

7

*"Be kind and compassionate to one another,
forgiving each other, just as in Christ God forgave you."*

Ephesians 4:32

Forgiveness is not always easy. It requires humility and grace, especially when we've been wronged or hurt. But as followers of Christ, we are called to emulate His love and forgiveness in our relationships with others, forgiving them even when it is the very last thing we wish to do.

When we forgive, we release the burden of bitterness and resentment, allowing God's peace to fill our hearts and minds. Forgiveness doesn't excuse the wrongdoing or erase the pain, but it frees us from being bound by it. It's a choice to let go of the past and move forward.

8

*"God is our refuge and strength,
an ever-present help in trouble."*

Psalm 46:1

God is our refuge—a safe haven where we can find shelter from life's storms. When adversity and hardship threaten to overwhelm us, we can take refuge in the unwavering presence of our Heavenly Father. He offers us a place of security and peace, where we can find rest for our weary souls and protection from the trials of life.

When we cry out to Him in distress, He hears our prayers and comes to our aid with unfailing love and compassion.

9

"From infancy you have known the holy Scriptures,
which are able to make you wise for salvation
through faith in Christ Jesus."

2 Timothy 3:15

In the Christian upbringing, Scripture is an ever-present part of life. From the earliest moments of our lives, the Word of God has the power to shape our hearts and minds, leading us to a deeper understanding of God's plan of salvation and His unfailing love for us.

Whether you have always lived a life of faith or are relatively new to the lifestyle, the holy words of the Bible can and should act as your guide, day by day, like a sort of manual to living with grace.

10

"When Jesus saw their faith, he said,
'Friend, your sins are forgiven.'"

Luke 5:20

In Luke 5:20, we witness a powerful moment where Jesus, moved by the faith of those who brought a paralyzed man to Him for healing, pronounces forgiveness over the man's sins. Jesus, in His infinite compassion and authority, addresses the man's most pressing need—forgiveness of sins.

In the same way, He sees our faith today and extends the same offer of forgiveness to each of us. No matter our circumstances or past mistakes, Jesus invites us to approach Him in faith, believing in His power to forgive and transform our lives.

11

"Cast your cares on the Lord and he will sustain you;
he will never let the righteous be shaken."

Psalm 55:22

Life often presents us with trials that can weigh heavily on our hearts and minds. We may find ourselves grappling with fear, uncertainty, or overwhelming circumstances. In such moments, it's natural to feel burdened and distressed. However, we don't have to carry these burdens alone. God generously invites us to unload our cares onto Him. He is our ever-present help in times of need, ready to shoulder our burdens and provide us with the strength and sustenance we require. When we surrender our worries to Him, we exchange our anxiety for His peace, our weakness for His strength, and our despair for His hope.

12

"Then I heard the voice of the Lord saying,
'Whom shall I send? And who will go for us?'
And I said, 'Here am I. Send me!'"

Isaiah 6:8

When we are called or asked to volunteer our time, efforts, or resources, it is easy to shrink back and wait for someone else to step up, shedding the responsibility from our shoulders. After all, there will always be someone else willing to help, right?

Our God expects more from us, His children. He expects us to be the first to step up, to offer ourselves in service of Him or of our fellow humans. Whether it is a calling or faith or of simple earthly matters, be that person who stands tall and sets an example for others.

13

*"I will praise the Lord, who counsels me;
even at night my heart instructs me."*

Psalm 16:7

In the quiet of the night, when the world around us settles into silence, the voice of God whispers gently to our hearts. His guidance transcends the boundaries of time, permeating every moment of our lives, even those when we sleep.

Consider the vast significance of God's counsel. His wisdom surpasses human understanding, and His guidance is perfect. Even when we are enveloped in darkness, uncertain of the path ahead, He remains our faithful guide. In the stillness of the night, He speaks to us, offering clarity and direction.

14

*"The Lord bless you and keep you; the Lord make
his face shine on you and be gracious to you;
the Lord turn his face toward you and give you peace."*

Numbers 6:24-26

In Numbers 6:24-26, we find one of the most beautiful and well-known blessings in the Bible. These words, spoken by God to Moses, were intended to be a blessing for the Israelites, but their significance extends far beyond that time and place. They are a timeless reminder of God's love, grace, and presence in our lives.

God's presence brings joy, hope, and abundant blessings into our lives. His face calms our fears, soothes our anxieties, and fills our hearts with contentment. And His spirit watches over us with unwavering care.

15

*"You are the light of the world.
A town built on a hill cannot be hidden."*

Matthew 5:14

Imagine a town perched atop a hill, its lights twinkling in the night sky for all to see. Such a town cannot be hidden; its radiance is unmistakable, drawing the attention of those near and far. Similarly, as bearers of Christ's light, we are called to stand out, to shine brightly in a world that often seems dimmed by despair and hopelessness.

Being a light of the world means living lives characterized by love, compassion, and integrity. It means speaking words of grace and truth, offering hope to the hopeless and comfort to the broken-hearted. It means walking in obedience to God's Word, even when it's countercultural or challenging.

16

*"And the peace of God, which transcends
all understanding, will guard your hearts
and your minds in Christ Jesus."*

Phillippians 4:7

In our busy and distracting lives, it's natural to overlook the importance of seeking God's counsel in every situation. Yet, Psalm 16:7 reminds us of the invaluable treasure we possess in His guidance. God's voice is always there, waiting and ready for us to listen. It may not come in audible words but in the gentle nudges of our hearts, in the peace that surpasses understanding, and in the quiet assurance that we are not forgotten.

June

17

"Let the peace of Christ rule in your hearts,
since as members of one body you were called to peace.
And be thankful."

Colossians 3:15

When we allow the peace of Christ to rule in our hearts, it not only transforms our individual lives but also influences the collective body of believers, creating an atmosphere of grace.

But how do we allow the peace of Christ to rule in our hearts? It begins with surrender—yielding our anxieties, worries, and fears to Him. It involves cultivating a deep and intimate relationship with Jesus through prayer, Scripture, and fellowship with other believers. As we immerse ourselves in His presence, His peace begins to permeate every aspect of our lives, guiding our thoughts, emotions, and actions.

18

"Even when I am old and gray, do not forsake me,
my God, till I declare your power to the next generation,
your mighty acts to all who are to come."

Psalm 71:18

As we journey through life, our physical strength may diminish and our outward appearance may show signs of aging. Yet, even in the midst of these changes, our God remains constant and unchanging. He is the same yesterday, today, and forever and His faithfulness endures through every season of life.

Regardless of our age or stage in life, we are called to be faithful stewards of the faith, sharing with others the incredible ways God has worked in our lives.

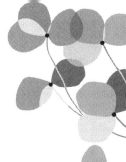

19

"I have told you these things,
so that in me you may have peace.
In this world you will have trouble.
But take heart! I have overcome the world."

John 16:33

In the midst of turmoil and uncertainty, where can we find true peace?

Jesus acknowledges the reality of hardship in this world. He doesn't promise us a life free from difficulties. Instead, He assures us that trouble will come. However, He doesn't leave us without hope. He offers something far greater—His peace.

When we fix our eyes on Jesus, our troubles fade in comparison to His overwhelming presence and power.

20

"'For I know the plans I have for you,' declares the Lord,
'plans to prosper you and not to harm you,
plans to give you hope and a future.'"

Jeremiah 29:11

"For I know the plans I have for you," declares the Lord. These words remind us that our lives are not governed by chance or circumstance but by the intentional and sovereign plans of a loving Heavenly Father. God is intimately acquainted with every detail of our lives, and His plans for us are filled with purpose and promise.

His plans for us extend far beyond the present—they encompass eternity. Even when we cannot see the way forward, we can trust that God is leading us toward a destiny far greater than we could ever imagine.

June

21

*"Be completely humble and gentle;
be patient, bearing with one another in love."*

Ephesians 4:2

Humility lies at the heart of Christian virtue, serving as the foundation upon which all other virtues are built. It involves recognizing our own limitations, acknowledging our need for God's grace, and esteeming others above ourselves. When we cultivate humility in our hearts, we create an environment where grace and compassion can flourish.

Similarly, patience requires endurance and forbearance, especially in the midst of challenging circumstances or difficult relationships.

Master these virtues and you will be that much closer to emulating the character of Christ in all that you do.

22

*"To the thirsty I will give water without cost
from the spring of the water of life."*

Revelation 21:6

The remarkable thing about God's offer of water from the spring of life is that it is freely given to all who come to Him in faith. This is grace in its purest form—a gift that cannot be earned but is freely bestowed out of God's boundless love for His creation.

The water of life that God offers is not merely a temporary fix or a fleeting pleasure. It is a source of eternal refreshment and renewal, springing forth from the very heart of God Himself. This water quenches the thirst of the soul like nothing else can, bringing healing, restoration, and abundant life.

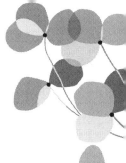

23

*"Do not be like them, for your Father knows
what you need before you ask him."*

Matthew 6:8

By "them," Jesus refers to the prayers of the Gentiles, who rely on lengthy repetitions and empty words. Unlike them, we believers know that what God values is the simple, heartfelt prayers of His followers. At the heart of this teaching lies a foundational truth: our Heavenly Father knows our needs even before we articulate them in prayer.

The fact that God knows our needs before we ask does not negate the importance of prayer. Rather, it underscores the beauty of our relationship with Him. Prayer, a means by which we deepen our intimacy with Him and surrender our concerns into His loving care.

24

*"Lord, I know that people's lives are not their own;
it is not for them to direct their steps."*

Jeremiah 10:23

This is an incredibly powerful acknowledgment by Jeremiah, who humbly accepts the limitations of human wisdom and understanding, recognizing that our lives are not ours to control.

We are ultimately creatures in need of divine guidance. Despite our best efforts and intentions, we are prone to wander off course, veering into paths of self-destruction and folly. Yet, when we acknowledge our need for God's direction, we open ourselves to His leading and guidance.

25

"The Lord has done it this very day;
let us rejoice today and be glad."

Psalm 118:24

In this Psalm, we find an invitation to rejoice and be glad in the Lord's daily provision and faithfulness. Each day is a gift from God, filled with His blessings, mercies, and grace.

Every moment, every blessing, every answered prayer is a testimony to His faithfulness and goodness. Nothing happens by chance or coincidence; rather, each day is orchestrated by the loving hand of our Heavenly Father.

Therefore, let us not take God's blessings for granted but instead, pause to acknowledge His goodness and faithfulness each day.

26

"The Lord is not slow in keeping his promise, as some
understand slowness. He is patient with you, not wanting
anyone to perish, but everyone to come to repentance."

2 Peter 3:9

Sometimes, as we wait for God to fulfill His promises, it may seem as though He is slow to act. We may grow impatient, questioning whether He will come through for us. Yet, Peter reassures us that God's timing is never delayed or deficient. He is faithful to His word, and His promises are sure, even if they are not fulfilled according to our timetable.

Instead, understand that this perceived delay is in fact a grace extended to us by God, giving us the opportunity to reach full and complete repentance, cleansing our souls, and embracing His path.

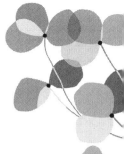

27

*"It is for freedom that Christ has set us free.
Stand firm, then, and do not let yourselves be
burdened again by a yoke of slavery."*

Galatians 5:1

The freedom we have in Christ is not merely freedom from external constraints or oppression, but freedom at the deepest level of our being. It is freedom from the power of sin, freedom from the bondage of the law, and freedom from the fear of condemnation.

In gratitude for this freedom, we are commanded to take responsibility for our facility and ensure that we are never again enslaved by mundane or material things.

28

*"For you have been born again, not of perishable seed,
but of imperishable, through the living and
enduring word of God."*

1 Peter 1:23

Peter compares the perishable nature of earthly things with the imperishable nature of the spiritual rebirth that comes through living in God's truth. Through the regenerating work of the Holy Spirit, believers are made new, transformed from spiritual death to spiritual life. This new birth marks the beginning of a lifelong journey of growth and sanctification in Christ. We are lucky to bear fruit that will last for eternity, bringing glory and honor to our Heavenly Father.

29

"Remind the people to be subject to rulers and authorities,
to be obedient, to be ready to do whatever is good,
to slander no one, to be peaceable and considerate,
and always to be gentle toward everyone."

Titus 3:1–2

In essence, this verse encourages us to live as ambassadors of Christ, embodying His love and grace in our conduct towards both believers and unbelievers alike. By embracing humility, obedience, and a commitment to goodness, we reflect the transformative power of Christ's presence in our lives.

Being subject to rulers and authorities doesn't just refer to obeying laws but also respecting structures in society. It's about being responsible citizens who contribute positively to the communities we're part of. It's our way of living in harmony within our world and channeling peace and security to our closest circles.

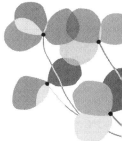

30

*"I know what it is to be in need, and I know what it is
to have plenty. I have learned the secret of being content
in any and every situation, whether well fed or hungry,
whether living in plenty or in want."*

Philippians 4:12

Paul's life was marked by extremes—he experienced seasons of abundance and seasons of lack, moments of plenty and moments of need. Yet, through it all, he discovered the secret of true contentment—not in his external circumstances, but in his relationship with Jesus Christ.

Paul's journey toward contentment was not instantaneous—it was a process of learning and growth. Likewise, finding contentment in our own lives requires intentional effort and a willingness to surrender our desires and expectations to God. It means choosing to trust Him even when our circumstances seem uncertain or challenging.

July

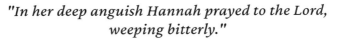

1

*"In her deep anguish Hannah prayed to the Lord,
weeping bitterly."*

1 Samuel 1:10

The story of Hannah offers us a glimpse into the power of prayer in the midst of deep sorrow. Hannah's longing for a child was met with years of infertility, causing her profound emotional pain. Yet, in the depths of her anguish, Hannah turned to the Lord in prayer.

Like Hannah, there may be times in our lives when we are confronted with grief. In these moments, we may find it difficult to articulate our prayers or make sense of our emotions. Yet, we can take comfort in knowing that God hears the cries of His children, even when our words fail us.

2

*"Do not be afraid, little flock, for your Father
has been pleased to give you the kingdom."*

Luke 12:32

Jesus addresses His disciples, affectionately referring to them as a "little flock." This notion of the Lord being a shepherd to guide us is a charming image of our relationship with Him.

A shepherd not only cares for his flock and leads them to safe grounds and abundant pastures, he truly loves them. He has a deep connection with each one, recognizes immediately when one has strayed off the beaten path and sees them as his own.

So are we cared for and beloved by our Heavenly Father, our shepherd in the pastures of life.

3

"Watch out that you do not lose what we have worked for, but that you may be rewarded fully."

2 John 1:8

The apostle John urges us to be vigilant in guarding the spiritual inheritance we have received. He cautions against complacency and warns against the potential loss of the blessings and rewards that come from faithful obedience to God.

Our labor in the Lord is not in vain; God promises to reward those who faithfully serve Him and endure to the end. Our reward may not always be immediate or tangible in this life, but it is assured in the life to come.

4

"But as for me and my house, we will serve the Lord."

Joshua 24:15

No matter how strong a foundation of faith we have built in our lives, we are constantly surrounded by reminders of a world without faith. We see it around us, in the media, on TV, in reading material. The pull to a secular world can sometimes feel strong, causing us to stop and think, "Do I really want this life of faith?"

The true test of faith is standing strong in the face of these distractions. Others may choose the path of lesser meaning, and that is their prerogative. But as for me and my family? We will choose the Lord, every single time.

July

5

*"You do not stay angry forever
but delight to show mercy."*

Micah 7:18

One of our greatest vices as humans is the grudges we bear and our inability to forgive lightly. These grudges burrow deep, gnawing at our souls and preventing us from reaching pure righteousness.

But God in His holiness suffers from no such corruption. Instead, He rejoices in showing mercy, in wiping our sins and wrongdoings from memory. He bears us no grudges and is always ready and willing to accept us in His arms.

6

*"And we know that in all things God works for
the good of those who love him, who have been
called according to his purpose."*

Romans 8:28

The key to experiencing the fullness of God's goodness in our lives is found in our love for Him. When our hearts are surrendered to God, when we seek to live in obedience to His Word, and we surrender to His purpose, we position ourselves to receive the blessings He has in store for us.

We can rest assured that God works day and night to do good to those who love and accept Him. When you accept Him truly in your heart, you are deserving of every wonderful thing He will bestow upon you.

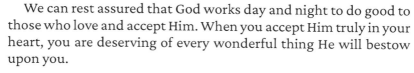

7

*"Come to me, all you who are weary and burdened,
and I will give you rest."*

Matthew 11:28

Sometimes, all we need is a breather. When life gets overwhelming, when our head is swimming with thoughts, to-do lists, worries, and distractions, we wish we could simply put our heads down and rest for a few minutes.

The beauty of cultivating a relationship with God is that this sense of rest and recuperation can be achieved through Him, deep in our hearts. When we unload our mental burdens on Him, He rests our souls and returns them fresh and new.

8

*"Command those who are rich in this present world
not to be arrogant nor to put their hope in wealth,
which is so uncertain, but to put their hope in God,
who richly provides us with everything for our enjoyment."*

1 Timothy 6:17

We often measure success by material wealth. Yet, these things are ultimately temporary and can never provide true fulfillment or security. Wealth can vanish in an instant, and the pursuit of riches can lead to arrogance and misplaced priorities.

Instead, let us understand that the richness we have in God is far greater than any riches we might acquire on Earth. When we recognize that everything we have is a gift, we can enjoy His blessings with gratitude and humility.

9

*"Teach the older women to be reverent in the way they live,
not to be slanderers or addicted to much wine,
but to teach what is good."*

Titus 2:3

This verse is amusing in its specificity, but when you take time to consider it, it can be an important teaching moment.

We should challenge ourselves to live lives of reverence and wisdom, regardless of our age or stage in life. May we be mindful of the example we are setting for those around us, and may we strive to live in a manner that brings glory to God.

10

*"The Lord your God is with you, the Mighty Warrior who
saves. He will take great delight in you; in his love he will no
longer rebuke you, but will rejoice over you with singing."*

Zephaniah 3:17

This verse offers a profound glimpse into the heart of God—a heart filled with love, compassion, and joy for His beloved children. It reminds us that God is not an impersonal or distant force but a loving Father who intimately knows and cares for each one of us. He delights in us, not because of anything we have done to earn His favor, but simply because we are His.

11

"Blessed is the one who perseveres under trial because, having stood the test, that person will receive the crown of life that the Lord has promised to those who love him."

James 1:12

Trials come in various forms—difficult circumstances, personal struggles, everyday routine, and more. Yet, rather than being occasions for despair or defeat, trials present opportunities for growth, refinement, and ultimately, blessing.

When we persevere under trial, clinging to God's promises and relying on His strength, we become stronger, more resilient, and better equipped to handle struggles in our future.

12

"Go and enjoy choice food and sweet drinks, and send some to those who have nothing prepared. This day is holy to our Lord. Do not grieve, for the joy of the Lord is your strength."

Nehemiah 8:10

In Nehemiah 8:10, we find a beautiful invitation to celebrate and share God's blessings with others. The act of sharing food and drink with others goes beyond mere provision; it is a tangible expression of love and care, a way of acknowledging the dignity and worth of every individual.

Generosity with the gifts we have been given by God is expected of us devout Christians. After all, we are God's messengers on Earth, and through us, His goodness is channeled.

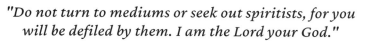

13

"Do not turn to mediums or seek out spiritists, for you will be defiled by them. I am the Lord your God."

Leviticus 19:31

This verse underscores the importance of trusting in the Lord alone for guidance, wisdom, and provision. God desires His people to rely on His Word rather than seeking answers from external sources. He alone is the source of truth and light, and any attempt to glean truth from mediums will be in vain.

Instead of turning to occult practices, God calls us to seek Him in prayer, study His Word, and unite with other believers.

14

"There is no God like you in heaven above or on earth below—you who keep your covenant of love with your servants who continue wholeheartedly in your way."

1 Kings 8:23

The covenant of love between God and His people is a central theme throughout the Bible and in Christian life. It is based on God's unchanging character and His commitment to His chosen ones. Despite the shortcomings and failures of humanity, God remains faithful to His promises, showering His people with His love, mercy, and grace. In return, we surrender our lives completely to Him, allowing His love to transform us from the inside out.

15

"Whoever pursues righteousness and love finds life, prosperity and honor."

Proverbs 21:21

The promise of Proverbs 21:21 is that those who diligently pursue righteousness and love will find life, prosperity, and honor. This does not necessarily mean a life free from hardship or struggle, but rather a life that is rich in the blessings of God's presence and favor.

Life in its fullest sense—abundant, meaningful, and eternal—is found in relationship with God through Jesus Christ. As we pursue righteousness and love, we experience the fullness of life that comes from knowing and walking with our Savior.

16

"Repent, for the kingdom of heaven has come near."

Matthew 3:2

Repentance is a central theme throughout Scripture that involves a change of heart and mind—a recognition of our need for forgiveness. Repentance is not a one-time event but an ongoing process of transformation as we continually surrender our lives to God.

The call to repentance is an invitation to turn from our sin and selfishness and instead find forgiveness, grace, and restoration in the loving arms of our Heavenly Father.

July

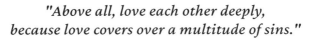

17

"Above all, love each other deeply,
because love covers over a multitude of sins."

1 Peter 4:8

We know that love is a crucial part of Christian life. We are called to selflessly and unconditionally love one another, indeed, above all else.

What is perhaps most striking about this verse is the statement that love covers over a multitude of sins. This does not mean that love overlooks or excuses sin, but rather that it has the power to reconcile and restore relationships that have been broken by sin. Love has the capacity to forgive, to heal, and to bridge the gaps that sin and hurt create between us.

18

"The Lord our God is merciful and forgiving,
even though we have rebelled against him."

Daniel 9:9

We see countless examples of God's mercy and forgiveness extended to His people. From the days of the Old Testament to the present age, God has consistently shown compassion and grace to those who turn to Him in repentance and faith.

No mortal man or woman, no matter how hard they may try, has the capacity to be so entirely and completely devoted to forgiveness. But we owe it to ourselves, to our loved ones, and to God, to do our best to steer our lives with compassion and mercy.

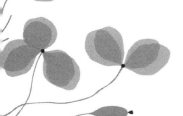

19

*"In my distress I called to the Lord, and he answered me.
From deep in the realm of the dead I called for help,
and you listened to my cry."*

Jonah 2:1-2

J onah's story is a memorable one, often taught to children. The
giant fish, the man swallowed whole, and the ultimate happy
ending make for a great tale.

But looking deeper into the Scripture, we realize that Jonah's
story was one of life or death. He was at the point of utter hopelessness, facing death itself. Yet, even in this dire circumstance, Jonah
recognized the power and compassion of God to save him.

Just as Jonah was eventually delivered safely from the belly of the
fish, so can we count on prayer to lead us out of difficult situations,
both big and small.

20

"Look to the Lord and his strength; seek his face always."

1 Chronicles 16:11

L ooking to the Lord is more than just a passing glance every once
in a while; it's a deliberate turning of our hearts toward Him,
regularly acknowledging His presence. In it, we find the renewal
of our strength, for He is the source of all power and might. When
we feel weak, His strength becomes our anchor, holding us steady
through whichever storm we face.

In seeking His face, we express to Him our yearning for His closeness and comfort. In this, we strengthen our bond with Him and
are awarded some of His own strength.

July

21

"Learn to do right; seek justice.
Defend the oppressed. Take up the cause of the fatherless;
plead the case of the widow."

Isaiah 1:17

Not everyone in this world around us is as fortunate as we are. We each come from a certain background with a specific set of circumstances, for better or worse. No matter where we are in life, we must always be intentional about seeking out those who are less fortunate and sharing our blessings with them.

It is God's will that we take under our wing those who are struggling or oppressed, and seek justice and fairness for their cause, even if it is not ours to fight for.

22

"Let us not become weary in doing good, for at the proper
time we will reap a harvest if we do not give up."

Galatians 6:9

In the journey of faith, there are moments when the tasks before us seem daunting, and the road ahead appears long and arduous. We do not always see the immediate results of our actions, but Galatians 6:9 reminds us that even so, we must persevere in doing what we know is right.

So push through, keep pressing forward in your commitment to live a life that honors God, and eventually, you will be generously rewarded.

23

*"It is easier for a camel to go through the eye of a needle
than for a rich man to enter the kingdom of God."*

Mark 10:25

This is perhaps an amusing comparison to imagine, but a powerful one nonetheless. It is clear that a creature as large as a camel has no hope of passing through a space so minute as the eye of a simple sewing needle.

In the same way, the Bible addresses the pursuit of wealth and possessions. It is not that wealth itself is inherently evil, but rather the pursuit of money above all else that can lead us astray. When our hearts are consumed by the desire for earthly treasures, it becomes nearly impossible to surrender to God fully.

24

*"Your statutes, Lord, stand firm;
holiness adorns your house for endless days."*

Psalm 93:5

God's holiness is not transient or temporary but enduring and everlasting. It adorns His house for endless days, filling every corner with His purity, righteousness, and glory.

No matter what objections or persecution our religion and faith may face, we know in our hearts that the reality of God will persevere. Whenever there have been people, there have been believers.

We are those people today, prolonging and perpetuating God's kingdom and His holy house, and in that, we should take pride.

25

"May the righteous be glad and rejoice before God; may they be happy and joyful."

Psalm 68:3

As righteous followers of Christ, we have reason to rejoice continually. Our joy isn't dependent on external circumstances but rooted in the knowledge of God and His promises. Even when we face trials, we can find joy in knowing that God is with us, working all things for our benefit.

When we partake in this joy, we become beacons of light and hope to those around us, pointing others toward the only source of true happiness and fulfillment.

26

"I have been crucified with Christ and I no longer live, but Christ lives in me."

Galatians 2:20

This important declaration of Paul's teaches us what happens when someone places their faith in Christ. When we open our hearts to Jesus and accept Him as our savior, our mortal lives become merely one facet of our being.

Our true self lies beyond our mortal body because He is within us. We are blessed with immortality and an existence beyond the physical, a blessing bestowed upon us in appreciation of our faith.

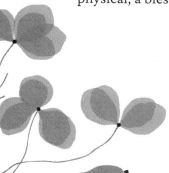

27

"Woe to him who builds his house by unjust gain,
setting his nest on high to escape the clutches of ruin!"

Habakkuk 2:9

The imagery of setting one's nest on high symbolizes a false sense of security and self-sufficiency. It's a picture of someone who trusts in their own abilities and resources rather than relying on God for provision and protection.

But we know, deep in our hearts, that there is no running from Him. Instead, we must run *to* Him, embracing His love with our whole hearts. Let us examine our hearts and motives, making sure that we are building our lives on the solid ground of God's truth.

28

"God is not human, that he should lie,
not a human being, that he should change his mind."

Numbers 23:19

We sometimes make the mistake of attributing human virtues to our Heavenly Father. We describe Him with words that we know, but in truth, God is above every human failing and struggle. In His divine perfection, he has no need to lie or deceive, nor does He change His mind like we do. His intentions are steadfast and calculated and every single thing He does has a reason.

All that remains for us is to trust in Him with all our heart, knowing that however it may seem, He has a plan for us.

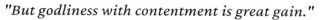

29

"But godliness with contentment is great gain."

1 Timothy 6:6

The Apostle Paul, writing to Timothy, reminds us that true wealth isn't measured by the size of our bank accounts or the abundance of our possessions. Instead, it's found a heart that is content with what God has provided.

In a world that is constantly offering newer, shinier things, it is no simple feat to be content with what you have. Learning to appreciate what you have, both in the physical world and the spiritual one, is one of the highest levels of godliness we can achieve.

30

"I will give you a new heart and put a new spirit in you;
I will remove from you your heart of stone
and give you a heart of flesh."

Ezekiel 36:26

A heart of stone is unyielding, stubborn, and resistant to God's will. It's incapable of experiencing true intimacy with Him or responding to His love and grace.

But God, in His boundless mercy and love, offers the gift of a new heart—a heart that is open to His guidance and receptive to His voice. This new heart is empowered by His Spirit, enabling us to love as He loves, to forgive as He forgives, and to live in obedience to His commands.

31

*"Let the message of Christ dwell among you richly
as you teach and admonish one another with all wisdom
through psalms, hymns, and songs from the Spirit,
singing to God with gratitude in your hearts."*

Colossians 3:16

What does it mean for the message of Christ to dwell among us richly? It means allowing the truths of the gospel to permeate every aspect of our lives—our thoughts, our attitudes, and our actions. It means immersing ourselves in the Word of God and allowing it to take root in our hearts.

We are called to teach one another with wisdom, using psalms, hymns, and spiritual song to encourage one another. Our gatherings are to be characterized by mutual instruction, accountability, and encouragement as we journey together in faith.

August

1

"But those who hope in the Lord will renew their strength. They will soar on wings like eagles; they will run and not grow weary, they will walk and not be faint."

Isaiah 40:31

When we place our hope in the Lord, something remarkable happens—we are infused with divine strength. It's a strength that enables us to rise above our circumstances, to overcome obstacles, and to persevere through trials. Like eagles soaring in the wind, we are empowered to navigate life's challenges with grace and resilience.

And even in everyday moments, we discover that our strength is continually renewed. We walk with confidence and steadfastness, knowing that God's presence guides our steps and sustains us along the way.

2

"My son, if sinful men entice you, do not give in to them."

Proverbs 1:10

The book of Proverbs is filled with practical wisdom, often conveyed through the fatherly advice given to a son. In this verse, the father urges his son to exercise caution and discernment when confronted with the enticing words and actions of sinful men.

Temptation may promise pleasure, success, or fulfillment, but ultimately leads to destruction and heartache.

So, we are called to be vigilant and discerning, recognizing and refusing to succumb to the lure of sin. Instead, we are to hold fast to the truth of God's Word and the guidance of His Spirit, which empowers us to resist temptation and continue to walk in righteousness.

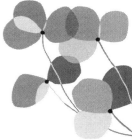

3

"But you are a chosen people, a royal priesthood,
a holy nation, God's special possession,
that you may declare the praises of him who called you
out of darkness into his wonderful light."

1 Peter 2:9

We have been chosen by God—not by our own merit or strength, but by His grace and love. We are handpicked by the Creator of the universe to be His own, to be part of His family and kingdom. We have the privilege of bringing our prayers, praises, and offerings directly to Him, serving as intermediaries between God and humanity.

And most amazingly, we are God's special possession, treasured and valued by Him above all else.

4

"She is more precious than rubies;
nothing you desire can compare with her."

Proverbs 3:15

This verse praises and glorifies the wonders of a wise, faithful woman. Such a woman is precious to those around her—her family, her friends, and everyone whose lives she touches.

Far more lovely and worthwhile than simple jewels or possessions, a loving, caring, kind woman who operates in wisdom and follows God's word brings a multitude of blessings and good fortune to her loved ones. Remember that when you doubt your worth—you are without a doubt, the most precious thing in this world.

August

5

*"The Lord is trustworthy in all he promises
and faithful in all he does."*

Psalm 145:13

Throughout Scripture, we encounter countless examples of God's faithfulness to His people. From the promises made to Abraham and the Israelites to the fulfillment of prophecy in the life, death, and resurrection of Jesus Christ, God has consistently proven Himself faithful and true.

We can take comfort in the faithfulness of God, reflect on His past faithfulness in our lives and in the lives of others, and let it serve as a source of hope and encouragement for the future. And may we live each day with the assurance that our God is trustworthy in all He promises and faithful in all He does.

6

"Everything is possible for one who believes."

Mark 9:23

These powerful words are a striking reminder of the effect of faith. When we believe, we tap into the boundless resources of God's strength and wisdom. Mountains that once seemed insurmountable become opportunities for God to display His miraculous power. Dreams that once appeared out of reach suddenly become within our grasp.

Challenge yourself to cultivate a deeper sense of belief in God and His promises. Instead of listening to voices of doubt and fear, replace them with the truth of God's Word.

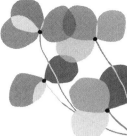

7

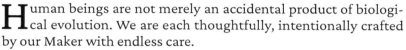

"For we are God's handiwork, created in Christ Jesus to do good works, which God prepared in advance for us to do."

Ephesians 2:10

Human beings are not merely an accidental product of biological evolution. We are each thoughtfully, intentionally crafted by our Maker with endless care.

Nothing about us is a mistake, nor are we anything but perfect in His eyes. In return, we must respect our bodies, love them, treat them well, and use them to do the good works for which we were intended, never straying from a path of righteousness and faith.

8

"Jesus would not entrust himself to them, for he knew all people. He did not need any testimony about mankind, for he knew what was in each person."

John 2:24-25

Despite the outward appearances of those around Him, Jesus knew the true condition of their hearts. He understood the complexities of human nature and the depths of our need for Him. He knew the hearts of all people intimately, and He was aware of His purpose and mission on earth—to seek and save the lost, to bring healing and restoration, and to offer salvation to all who believed in Him.

He sees us, each day, for who we truly are. There is no need to hide our flaws from Him, because He sees and loves us despite them all.

August

9

"You will keep in perfect peace those whose minds are steadfast, because they trust in you."

Isaiah 26:3

The key to experiencing perfect peace lies in having steadfast minds—minds that are firmly anchored in God's truth and unwavering in their trust in Him. When our minds are steadfastly fixed on God, we are awarded with a deep sense of calm and assurance that comes from knowing that God is in control and that His purposes will ultimately prevail.

10

"Now he who supplies seed to the sower and bread for food will also supply and increase your store of seed and will enlarge the harvest of your righteousness."

2 Corinthians 9:10

This verse speaks not only to material blessings but also to the spiritual growth and fruitfulness that result from a life lived in obedience to God.

God is the ultimate provider. He is the one who supplies the seed for sowing and the bread for sustenance. He gives to us generously, never failing in his kindness.

As He blesses us, He entrusts us with even greater opportunities to be a blessing to others, to share His love and grace with those around us.

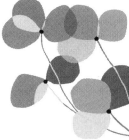

11

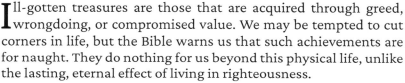
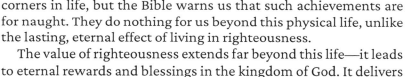

"Ill-gotten treasures have no lasting value,
but righteousness delivers from death."

Proverbs 10:2

Ill-gotten treasures are those that are acquired through greed, wrongdoing, or compromised value. We may be tempted to cut corners in life, but the Bible warns us that such achievements are for naught. They do nothing for us beyond this physical life, unlike the lasting, eternal effect of living in righteousness.

The value of righteousness extends far beyond this life—it leads to eternal rewards and blessings in the kingdom of God. It delivers us from the consequences of sin and death, offering us the hope of salvation and the promise of eternal life with Him.

12

"Therefore, if anyone is in Christ, the new creation
has come: The old has gone, the new is here!"

2 Corinthians 5:17

When we enter into relationship with Christ, we become new creations—our old way of life is replaced by a new way of living in Him. This is true whether we are accepting Jesus in our lives for the very first time, or returning to Him after a period of distance.

The old has gone—our sins, our past mistakes, our failures— they are all washed away by the blood of Jesus. We are no longer defined by our past, but by our identity in Christ. We are forgiven, redeemed, and set free from the bondage of sin and death.

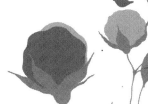

13

"I have fought the good fight,
I have finished the race, I have kept the faith."

2 Timothy 4:7

Paul compares his journey of faith with a race—a metaphor that highlights the perseverance, endurance, and determination required to navigate the Christian life. Throughout his ministry, Paul faced persecution, opposition, and hardships of every kind, yet he remained steadfast in his devotion to Christ.

May these words inspire us to press on in our own journey of faith with renewed determination and resolve. May we fight the good fight, finish the race, and keep the faith, knowing that our labor in the Lord is not in vain.

14

"Truly I tell you, if you have faith as small as a mustard seed,
you can say to this mountain, 'Move from here to there,'
and it will move. Nothing will be impossible for you."

Matthew 17:20

Faith, no matter how small or seemingly insignificant, has the potential to move mountains and accomplish the impossible. When we nurture our faith with prayer, devotion, and obedience, we allow it to grow and flourish.

The more we care for our faith and work at it, the more we are able to accomplish with it. If faith as small as a mustard seed can move mountains, imagine what a whole life of faithful devotion can produce!

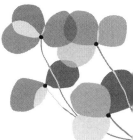

15

*"Therefore encourage one another and build each other up,
just as in fact you are doing."*

1 Thessalonians 5:11

We live in a community and are part of many bigger circles of people. We do not live in our own little world, and as such, we have a duty to be mindful of those around us and how they are.

God commands us to actively partake in the encouragement of others, to put our own vitality and mood to use to help others, encouraging them and building them up to be people of faith and righteousness.

16

*"One thing I ask from the Lord, this only do I seek:
that I may dwell in the house of the Lord all the days
of my life, to gaze on the beauty of the Lord
and to seek him in his temple."*

Psalm 27:4

To dwell in the house of the Lord is not merely about physical proximity but about experiencing the intimacy of His presence. It's about cultivating a deep and abiding relationship with Him, where we find solace, strength, and satisfaction for our souls.

The temple where we may seek him is deep in our own hearts, an intangible place of worship we can go to at any time. There, we can observe and learn from His eternal beauty and wisdom.

17

*"Therefore I tell you, do not worry about your life,
what you will eat or drink; or about your body,
what you will wear. Is not life more than food,
and the body more than clothes?"*

Matthew 6:25

Matthew 6:25 serves as a gentle reminder from Jesus Himself to trust in God's provision and not to be consumed by worry and anxiety about our material needs.

At the heart of Jesus' teaching is a call to trust. He invites us to place our confidence in the goodness and faithfulness of our Heavenly Father, who knows our needs even before we ask Him. When we release our worries into His hands, we experience the peace in knowing that He is in control and that He cares for us deeply.

18

*"Be on your guard; stand firm in the faith;
be courageous; be strong."*

1 Corinthians 16:13

Four important directives are given to us in this short verse. "Be on your guard"—be vigilant in the face of temptation, guarding our hearts and minds with the truth of God's Word. "Stand firm in the faith"—do not take your faith lightly, but invest in it, building a strong and stable foundation. "Be courageous"—be willing to be vocal about your faith, even when you face opposition. Finally, "be strong"—learn to draw on God's power and resources, leaning on Him for support.

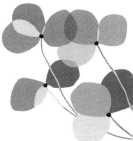

19

"Do everything without grumbling or arguing,
so that you may become blameless and pure, children
of God without fault in a warped and crooked generation.
Then you will shine among them like stars in the sky."

Philippians 2:14-15

The apostle Paul urges us to do everything without grumbling or arguing. This is a call to cultivate a spirit of contentment and gratitude, even in the midst of challenging circumstances or difficult relationships. When we choose to approach life with a positive attitude and a willingness to serve others, we become visible manifestations of God's grace and truth in a world that is desperately in need of both.

20

"Jesus looked at them and said, 'With man this is impossible,
but not with God; all things are possible with God.'"

Mark 10:27

Jesus contrasts the limitations of human effort with the boundless possibilities available through God. While we may encounter situations that are beyond our own abilities to solve or overcome, we can trust in the unfailing strength of our Heavenly Father. He is the One who can move mountains, part seas, and bring life out of death.

This truth should fill us with hope and confidence, knowing that we serve a God who specializes in the impossible. No challenge is too great, no problem too complex, and no situation too hopeless for Him to handle.

·August

21

*"We have sinned, even as our ancestors did;
we have done wrong and acted wickedly."*

Psalm 106:6

No one is free from sin. Our ancestors have sinned, we have sinned, and our descendants will sin as well—that is the reality of being humans.

If sin and wickedness are so inevitable, what is the point in even trying?

God knows that in our human imperfection, we cannot always be good. But He encourages us and expects us to face the challenge head on. The beauty is not being free of sin, but rather knowing that even when we do fall, we must get back up and amend our ways.

22

"For we live by faith, not by sight."

2 Corinthians 5:7

2 Corinthians 5:7 encapsulates the essence of the Christian life—a life characterized by complete trust in God, even when circumstances seem uncertain or difficult to understand. It challenges us to shift our focus from the physical realm to the spiritual reality of God's presence, something we are not necessarily accustomed to doing.

The journey of faith is not always easy. There will be times when we face challenges, doubts, and uncertainties along the way. But when we persevere in trusting God, we discover that He is faithful and will lead us through every trial and triumph.

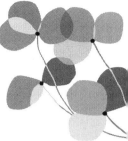

23

*"No wise man, enchanter, magician or diviner can
explain to the king the mystery he has asked about,
but there is a God in heaven who reveals mysteries."*

Daniel 2:27-28

There are mysteries in life that are beyond human comprehension. There are questions that science, philosophy, or human reasoning cannot fully answer. Yet, as believers, we take comfort in the knowledge that we serve a God who knows all things and holds all things in His hands.

God is not only the Creator of the universe but also the Revealer of secrets. He delights in unveiling His plans to those who seek Him and invites us to come to Him with our questions and uncertainties, knowing that He is able to provide the wisdom, insight, and understanding we need.

24

*"My comfort in my suffering is this:
Your promise preserves my life."*

Psalm 119:50

Suffering is a universal experience, one that touches every life at some point or another. Whether it be physical pain, emotional anguish, or spiritual turmoil, the weight of suffering can feel overwhelming. Yet, even in the darkest moments, we can find solace in the promises of God.

We can find hope in His assurances of love, grace, and redemption. And we can trust that His promises are sure and steadfast, enduring through every difficulty.

25

"Even in darkness light dawns for the upright,
for those who are gracious and
compassionate and righteous."

Psalm 112:4

There has never in history been a night not followed by dawn. Darkness can take many forms in our lives—it may be the darkness of grief, pain, uncertainty, fear, sin, shame, or despair. Yet, regardless of the nature of the darkness we face, the light of God's presence illuminates the path before us, guiding us through the darkest valleys and leading us into His light. It shines brightly in the hearts of the upright—those who are gracious, compassionate, and righteous—who reflect the character of God Himself.

26

"We love because he first loved us."

1 John 4:19

The Lord sets an example for us in all that He does. In every action and word, we can learn something about how to be better people, living lives of faith.

Perhaps His most shining example for us is His unwavering love for His children. He loved us so much that He gave us His only Son.

We, too, should learn from his guidance to commit ourselves to loving one another unashamedly and with no strings attached. For who are we to hate or be unkind to another one of God's many beloved children?

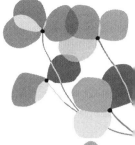

27

*"I will praise God's name in song
and glorify him with thanksgiving."*

Psalm 69:30

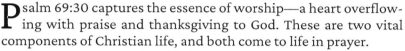

Psalm 69:30 captures the essence of worship—a heart overflowing with praise and thanksgiving to God. These are two vital components of Christian life, and both come to life in prayer.

When we pray, we should do so with enthusiasm and joy. We should sing, shout, and revel in His greatness, glorifying His name for all to hear. Allow your worship to flow from a heart overflowing with gratitude for who God is and all that He has done.

28

*"There is neither Jew nor Gentile,
neither slave nor free, nor is there male and female,
for you are all one in Christ Jesus."*

Galatians 3:28

In Christ, all barriers are broken down, and all believers are united as one family, sharing in the same inheritance and belonging to the same body. Our unity as Christians transcends social, cultural, and gender distinctions. There is no room for favoritism or exclusion. Instead, there is only love, acceptance, and equality for all who belong to Him.

August

29

*"Rejoice in the Lord always.
I will say it again: Rejoice!"*

Phillippians 4:4

The command to rejoice in the Lord always is not contingent upon our feelings or external factors. It's a choice—an intentional decision to fix our focus on the goodness, faithfulness, and sovereignty of God, even when life is difficult or uncertain.

Our joy is not dependent on fleeting emotions or temporary circumstances. No matter what trials or tribulations we may face, we can rejoice in the knowledge that God is with us, working all things together for our good and His glory.

30

*"Trust in the Lord with all your heart and lean
not on your own understanding; in all your ways submit
to him, and he will make your paths straight."*

Proverbs 3:5-6

Trusting in the Lord with all our heart means placing our full confidence and reliance on Him, even when we don't fully understand His ways or His plans for us. It's a recognition that God's ways are higher than our ways and His thoughts are higher than our thoughts, and that He alone knows what is best for us.

Trusting in God's guidance requires humility, faith, and obedience. It requires us to let go of our need for control. When we yield to His direction, we are rewarded with peace and fulfillment.

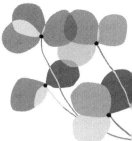

31

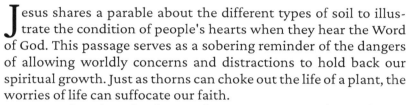

*"The seed falling among the thorns refers to
someone who hears the word, but the worries
of this life and the deceitfulness of wealth
choke the word, making it unfruitful."*

Matthew 13:22

Jesus shares a parable about the different types of soil to illus-
trate the condition of people's hearts when they hear the Word
of God. This passage serves as a sobering reminder of the dangers
of allowing worldly concerns and distractions to hold back our
spiritual growth. Just as thorns can choke out the life of a plant, the
worries of life can suffocate our faith.

To guard against the thorns of worry, we must cultivate hearts
that are rooted in faith and anchored in God's truth. We must fix
our eyes on Jesus and trust in Him.

September

1

"I thank Christ Jesus our Lord, who has given me strength, that he considered me faithful, appointing me to his service."

1 Timothy 1:12

Paul's acknowledgment of Christ's strength highlights an important truth for every believer: our ability to serve God effectively comes not from our own efforts or abilities, but from the empowering presence of Christ within us.

Therefore, let us acknowledge our dependence on Him for every good work and endeavor to serve Him faithfully with the gifts and abilities He has given us.

2

"Evildoers are trapped by their sinful talk, and so the innocent escape trouble."

Proverbs 12:13

Evildoers, through their sinful talk and actions, ultimately bring about their own downfall. Their malicious words and deeds ensnare them in trouble and lead to their own destruction.

On the other hand, the innocent—who walk in integrity and speak truthfully—find refuge from trouble. Their words are a source of blessing and protection, guiding them away from harm and leading them to safety. When temptation for evildoing inevitably calls, reflect upon this truth—which would you prefer to be?

3

"Your love has given me great joy
and encouragement, because you, brother,
have refreshed the hearts of the saints."

Philemon 1:7

When we extend love to our brothers and sisters in Christ, we not only bring joy and encouragement to them but also bring peace and renewal to their hearts and souls. Our words of affirmation, acts of service, and gestures of kindness toward others have the power to uplift and strengthen those around us, creating a sense of belonging and unity within the family of God.

4

"Your love has given me great joy
and encouragement, because you, brother,
have refreshed the hearts of the Lord's people."

Matthew 21:22

Prayer can sometimes seem insubstantial to fulfill our needs. We do not always have the privilege of hearing God's Word spoken to us, and it is easy to feel like our prayers are simply going unanswered.

But Matthew 21 reminds us of an important truth. No matter what we see or how we feel, if we are true and whole in our faith, our prayers will be answered. Perhaps not in the way or timing we expect, but certainly in the form that is best for us, true to God's divine plan.

September

5

*"For everyone who asks receives; the one who seeks finds;
and to the one who knocks, the door will be opened."*

Luke 11:10

There is so much to be learned from our rich history. The Bible is not merely a collection of ancient stories but a living and active word that speaks directly to our circumstances today. It contains timeless truths and principles that transcend time and culture, offering us wisdom and guidance for every aspect of life.

So, we must cherish the gift of Scripture and allow its timeless truths to shape and transform our lives, every single day.

6

"The Lord is my shepherd, I lack nothing."

Psalm 23:1

The imagery of God as a shepherd is rich with meaning and significance. A shepherd is responsible for guiding, protecting, and providing for the needs of his flock. In the same way, God shepherds His people with love, wisdom, and tender care, ensuring that we have everything that is essential for our well-being.

When we acknowledge the Lord as our shepherd, we affirm our dependence on Him. We trust in His ability to meet our needs and rest in the assurance that He is faithful to provide for us, both spiritually and materially, in abundance and in times of scarcity.

7

*"The Lord does not look at the things people look at.
People look at the outward appearance,
but the Lord looks at the heart."*

1 Samuel 16:7

There is a stark contrast between human and divine perception. While we often judge based on outward appearances, God sees beyond the surface to the very core of our being. He looks at the heart.

God's perspective challenges us to value what truly matters. For believers, this means cultivating inner qualities such as faith, humility, love, and obedience, which are pleasing to God. It means prioritizing character over appearance, integrity over image, and spiritual growth over worldly gain.

8

*"Laziness brings on deep sleep,
and the shiftless go hungry."*

Proverbs 19:15

In a world that often celebrates instant gratification, this verse is a reminder of the importance of hard work and perseverance. We are challenged to examine our own attitude toward productivity. Are we diligent in fulfilling our responsibilities and pursuing our goals, or do we succumb to laziness and procrastination? Are we willing to put in the effort and discipline required to achieve success, or do we expect things to be handed to us on a silver platter?

Let us commit ourselves to embracing diligence and hard work in every area of our lives.

9

*"See what great love the Father has lavished on us,
that we should be called children of God!
And that is what we are! The reason the world
does not know us is that it did not know him."*

1 John 3:1

The magnitude of God's love is revealed in our being called children of God. Through faith in Jesus Christ, we are adopted into God's family, welcomed with open arms, and embraced as beloved sons and daughters. This reality may be met with misunderstanding or rejection by the world around us, who may not understand because they do not know the One who has called us His own. But we can stand tall and sure of our position as His beloved people.

10

*"For everything that was written in the past
was written to teach us, so that through the endurance
taught in the Scriptures and the encouragement
they provide we might have hope."*

Romans 15:4

God is a loving and attentive Father who delights in responding to the needs of His children. Just as parents are eager to provide for the needs of their children, so too does our Heavenly Father desire to bless us and meet our needs.

So long as we persist in prayer, trusting in God's perfect timing and His infinite wisdom to answer according to His will, no prayer will go unanswered and no door will remain closed to us for long.

11

*"He gives strength to the weary and
increases the power of the weak."*

Isaiah 40:29

Life's journey can be exhausting. Yet, in the midst of our struggles, God offers us His strength—the kind of strength that sustains us, uplifts us, and empowers us to press on, no matter what we face.

If you find yourself feeling weary or weak, take heart in His promise. Know that God sees your struggles, understands your limitations, and is ready to give you the strength you need to carry on. Surrender your burdens to Him, lean on His grace, and trust in His power to carry you through every difficulty.

12

*"May God himself, the God of peace, sanctify you through
and through. May your whole spirit, soul and body be kept
blameless at the coming of our Lord Jesus Christ."*

1 Thessalonians 5:23

Paul addresses God as the "God of peace," emphasizing His role in bringing about our sanctification. True sanctification is not merely a human effort or self-improvement project; it is a work of God's grace and power in our lives. It is He who transforms us from the inside out, spirit, body, and soul.

May our entire being be kept blameless until the coming of our Lord Jesus Christ.

13

*"If you are returning to the Lord with all your hearts,
then rid yourselves of the foreign gods and the Ashtoreths
and commit yourselves to the Lord and serve him only."*

1 Samuel 7:3

Genuine repentance involves more than just words or outward actions; it requires a sincere turning of the heart back to God. It's a call to rid ourselves of anything that hinders our relationship with Him and to commit ourselves to Him wholeheartedly.

We cannot be fully in God when we place other things in higher priority to Him. He should be our single, true Father, whom we trust and believe in with all our hearts.

14

*"I thank God, whom I serve, as my ancestors did,
with a clear conscience, as night and day I constantly
remember you in my prayers."*

2 Timothy 1:3

Paul served God with dedication and sincerity, drawing inspiration from the faithful example of his ancestors who had gone before him. We, too, can learn from his example how to be faithful servants to the Lord. Let's commit ourselves to living with a clear conscience, honoring God in all that we do, and praying constantly for the well-being of others.

15

*"We were born only yesterday and know nothing,
and our days on earth are but a shadow."*

Job 8:9

In the grand scheme of eternity, our lives are a fleeting moment. Despite our accomplishments, knowledge, and experiences, which are important and appreciated, we are humbled by the realization that our understanding has its limits.

While our earthly lives may be brief, they are not without purpose or meaning. It is our privilege and responsibility to dedicate our lives to glorifying God and to leaving a lasting legacy for those who come after us.

16

*"Woe to those who make unjust laws, to those who issue
oppressive decrees, to deprive the poor of their rights and
withhold justice from the oppressed of my people."*

Isaiah 10:1-2

In every society, there are individuals who misuse power and authority for their own gain at the expense of others. As you reflect on this passage, examine your own life and attitudes towards justice and compassion. Are there ways you can use your influence and resources to advocate for those who are marginalized and oppressed?

Living a life of faith means devoting ourselves to seeking true justice at every turn and upholding compassion in our every word and action.

September

17

"I will show my greatness and my holiness, and I will make myself known in the sight of many nations. Then they will know that I am the Lord."

Ezekiel 38:23

Throughout history, God has demonstrated His greatness and holiness through His mighty works, His faithful promises, and His righteous judgments. From the parting of the Red Sea to the resurrection of Jesus Christ, God's acts of power and redemption have left a mark on the hearts and minds of people across generations and nations.

We are lucky to be His witnesses and messengers here on Earth, to help spread the word of His greatness and reveal His glory for all the world to know.

18

"Since they hated knowledge and did not choose to fear the Lord; since they would not accept my advice and spurned my rebuke, they will eat the fruit of their ways and be filled with the fruit of their schemes."

Proverbs 1:29-31

It's easy to become complacent with worldly knowledge and acceptance of the mundane. We may prefer to follow our own desires and impulses rather than submit to the wisdom of God's Word.

Yet, Proverbs warns us that the path of self-reliance and rebellion against God's ways leads only to destruction and despair. But God's desire is not for our destruction but for our redemption and restoration. When we choose the path of wisdom and obedience, we are all the more blessed for it.

19

"A generous person will prosper;
whoever refreshes others will be refreshed."

Proverbs 11:25

The reality of Christian life is that what we give, we ultimately receive in return. It may not be immediate and it may not even be clear to us, but we must trust that our hard work and generosity will be rewarded.

Being generous is more than just giving to others—it is doing so with grace and enthusiasm, and without inhibition. It means seeking out those situations in which our time, resources, or emotions can be spent giving to others and improving their situation.

When we give, our hearts fill and our souls rejoice.

20

"No one should seek their own good,
but the good of others."

1 Corinthians 10:24

Selfishness is a common temptation in the modern, individualistic world. However, as followers of Christ, we are called to a higher standard—a standard of selflessness and sacrificial love.

We are called to look out for others before ourselves, to work and toil for the good of others, putting their wellbeing before our own.

In a beautiful world, where we each care for others more than we care for ourselves, no one should ever lack for anything.

September

21

"He leads me beside quiet waters,
he restores my soul."

Psalm 23:2-3

The routine of life can be chaotic and demanding, a hustle and bustle of noise and distractions. It's natural to become overwhelmed, to feel spiritually depleted and emotionally drained.

When we allow God to lead us beside quiet waters, He provides us with a space to pause, to breathe, and to be still. It is a place where we can lay down our burdens, pour out our hearts, and find calm for our souls.

22

"Do not neglect your gift, which was given you through
prophecy when the body of elders laid their hands on you."

1 Timothy 4:14

We are all born with a unique set of gifts. These are our talents, our intelligence—both academic and emotional, our abilities, and our potential.

We each have different gifts, but we are all united in that these gifts were intentionally bestowed upon us by our loving Father, who sees us for who we are and knows the potential of our lives.

Throughout our lifetime, it is our duty to make the most of these God-given gifts—to nurture and feed them, working and practicing every day to deserve what we have been given.

23

*"Let the morning bring me word of your unfailing love,
for I have put my trust in you."*

Psalm 143:8

This psalm beautifully captures our longing for the assurance of God's unfailing love. It reflects a deep desire to awaken each morning with the comforting reminder of God's steadfast and unwavering devotion to us, which will carry us through the day.

The harder we work on our relationship with God and the more we invest into our faith, the more natural it will be for us to trust in His unflinching love.

When you are truly complete in your journey of faith, you will wake each morning knowing without a shred of doubt that He is with you, ready to set the tone for another wonderful day.

24

"I always thank my God as I remember you in my prayers."

Philemon 1:4–5

Prayer is a powerful and transformative act of communion with God, where we have the privilege of bringing our concerns, desires, and praises before Him. When we remember others in our prayers, we not only intercede on their behalf but also express our gratitude for the blessing they are to us.

Expressing gratitude in prayer not only honors God for His faithfulness in bringing these individuals into our lives but also strengthens our relationships with them. It fosters a spirit of appreciation, encouragement, and love as we acknowledge the ways they have enriched and impacted our journey of faith.

September

25

*"But the Lord is faithful, and he will strengthen you
and protect you from the evil one."*

2 Thessalonians 3:3

In this verse in Thessalonians, we are promised that the Lord will be with us, strengthening and protecting us from "the evil one." We all struggle with evil in our lives. What form does evil take in yours? It may manifest as temptation, greed, selfishness, or laziness. It may look different every single day.

Regardless, these evils are a foe for us to contend with, and we do not have to do so alone. Our loving Father is here for us, should we only open our hearts to Him.

26

*"Give proper recognition to those widows
who are really in need."*

1 Timothy 5:3

Widows in biblical times often faced hardships, left without the protection traditionally provided by their husbands. They were at risk of poverty, social isolation, and exploitation, making them particularly vulnerable within society.

Today, vulnerable people may look a little different. It could be someone struggling financially or mentally, someone lacking a strong and loving support system, or someone having difficulty with their faith. Those of us who live by faith are called upon to extend compassion and support to the marginalized, the oppressed, and the vulnerable among us, no matter who they are and what they look like.

27

"She opens her arms to the poor
and extends her hands to the needy."

Proverbs 31:20

Proverbs paints a portrait of a virtuous and noble woman whose character is marked by wisdom, strength, and compassion. Most importantly, we see here a striking depiction of her compassionate heart as she opens her arms to the poor and extends her hands to the needy.

Compassion lies at the core of the virtuous woman's character. She doesn't turn a blind eye to the struggles and hardships of those around her; instead, she actively seeks out opportunities to show kindness, generosity, and support to the less fortunate. Her heart is attuned to the needs of others, and she responds with empathy and action.

28

"Discretion will protect you,
and understanding will guard you."

Proverbs 2:11

Wise decision-making and discernment are invaluable assets that offer us protection and security. Discretion refers to the ability to make sound judgments and choices based on careful consideration and discernment. Understanding, on the other hand, encompasses a deeper knowledge and insight into the mysterious ways of God.

Together, these two act as safeguards for our words and lives, shielding us from harm and leading us on a path of faithfulness.

September

29

*"She is clothed with strength and dignity;
she can laugh at the days to come."*

Proverbs 31:25

Proverbs praises the strong woman whose character is marked by strength, dignity, and fearless confidence. She does not cower and fear the unknown future, but takes it on with enthusiasm and courage, certain of the virtue of her path.

We, too, should strive to be such a woman. One who puts her trust in Christ to the extent that she fears nearly nothing, who navigates her life with grace and determination, nurturing and lifting up those around her who bask in her light.

30

*"Teach the older men to be temperate,
worthy of respect, self-controlled, and sound in faith,
in love and in endurance."*

Titus 2:2

Titus 2:2 presents us with four important virtues that we, as faithful Christians, should strive to embody. These qualities are not only desirable but essential for living a life that honors God and influences others positively.

First, temperance calls for moderation and self-restraint in all areas of life. Secondly, being worthy of respect means conducting oneself in a manner that commands admiration and esteem from others. Next, self-control is essential for navigating life's challenges and temptations. And finally, being sound in faith, love, and endurance means having a firm and unwavering faith in God.

October

1

"All of you, clothe yourselves with humility toward one another, because, 'God opposes the proud but shows favor to the humble.'"

1 Peter 5:5

Humility is a virtue that lies at the heart of the Christian life. It involves recognizing our own limitations, weaknesses, and need for God's grace, as well as valuing others above ourselves. When we clothe ourselves with humility, we adopt an attitude of gentleness and respect in our interactions with others.

As we walk in humility, may we experience the abundant favor and blessings that come from living in alignment with God's will.

2

"Why should fools have money in hand to buy wisdom, when they are not able to understand it?"

Proverbs 17:16

The Bible paints fools as not merely those who lack intellectual capacity but those who reject wisdom and choose to live in rebellion against God's principles. They may possess material wealth, yet their hearts remain closed to the truths of God's Word and the guidance of His Spirit.

We must seek every day to ensure that our resources and wisdom go hand in hand - nourishing each other and living in harmony so that our understanding and reverence never waver.

3

"For I will forgive their wickedness
and will remember their sins no more."

Jeremiah 31:34

The forgiveness offered by God is a complete removal of our sins from His sight. When God forgives, He chooses to remember our sins no more, his forgiveness is thorough, absolute, and unconditional, offered to us freely.

If our sins against God can be so easily forgiven, who are we to bear grudges against those who have committed human sins against us? Let us learn from our Father the incredible grace that lies in letting go of hurt and healing our hearts.

4

"Finally, brothers and sisters, rejoice!
Strive for full restoration, encourage one another,
be of one mind, live in peace.
And the God of love and peace will be with you."

2 Corinthians 13:11

Paul calls us to rejoice, pursue unity, and live in peace. Despite the challenges and trials we may face, we have every reason to rejoice in the Lord. Our joy is not dependent on our circumstances but on our relationship with Christ, who is our source of hope, strength, and eternal salvation. Full restoration requires humility, forgiveness, and a willingness to extend grace to one another. And encouragement is the selfless act of offering words of affirmation, support, and comfort to others. Do all these, and God will surely be with you.

October

5

*"But as for me, I watch in hope for the Lord,
I wait for God my Savior; my God will hear me."*

Micah 7:7

The assurance that "my God will hear me" provides comfort and encouragement to us believers. It reminds us that our prayers are not uttered in vain but are heard by a loving and attentive God who will respond to the cries of His children. God's ears are open to the pleas of His people, and He is always ready to come to their aid.

As we wait patiently for Him, may we find strength and comfort in the knowledge that our God hears our prayers and is faithful to fulfill His promises in His perfect timing.

6

*"And everyone who calls on the name of the Lord
will be saved."*

Joel 2:32

This significant declaration offers any man, woman, and child access to God's graces. His love, forgiveness, and blessings are not reserved solely for those who have known and known Him from birth, but for all those who take it upon themselves to accept His presence in their life and to cry out His name.

Remember that no matter how distant you may feel from your faith and your path, all it takes is one call - a cry that will be answered by the Lord, as long as you are sincere in your plea.

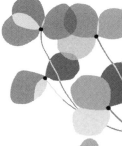

7

*"May the God of hope fill you with all joy and peace
as you trust in him, so that you may overflow
with hope by the power of the Holy Spirit."*

Romans 15:13

As we trust in God, our faith becomes the channel through which His joy flows into our hearts. This is a deep-seated joy that transcends the trials of life, grounded in the knowledge of God's faithfulness and promises.

When we open our hearts to Him, we can receive the abundant blessings of joy, peace, and hope that God offers us through His Holy Spirit.

8

*"Now the Lord is the Spirit, and where the Spirit
of the Lord is, there is freedom."*

2 Corinthians 3:17

The Spirit of the Lord brings freedom in multiple dimensions of our lives. Firstly, it brings freedom from the power of sin. Through God's strength, we are able to overcome the temptations and struggles that once held us captive.

Secondly, we are freed from fear and condemnation. In Christ, we are no longer bound by guilt and shame for our past mistakes and failures.

And lastly, the Spirit brings freedom to live out our God-given purpose and calling, to serve others and make a lasting impact for years to come.

9

"When we heard of it, our hearts melted in fear and everyone's courage failed because of you, for the Lord your God is God in heaven above and on the earth below."

Joshua 2:11

Rahab, a resident of Jericho, acknowledges the power and sovereignty of the God of Israel. Rahab's recognition of God's supremacy is a powerful reminder of His authority over all creation. There is no realm, no power, and no authority that can rival His majesty and dominion.

Rahab's confession serves as a call to trust in the Lord, even when circumstances seem overwhelming. Just as He was faithful to deliver Israel from their enemies, so too will He be faithful to guide and protect His people today.

10

"But when they cried out to the Lord, he raised up for them a deliverer."

Judges 3:9

We see a recurring theme throughout the book of Judges: the faithfulness of God to choose deliverers for His people in their time of need. Despite the repeated cycle of sin, oppression, and repentance among His people, God remained faithful to rescue them when they cried out to Him.

In the same way, may we never hesitate to turn to Him in times of trouble, knowing that He is always ready to extend His saving hand.

11

*"Take delight in the Lord,
and he will give you
the desires of your heart."*

Psalm 37:4

To "take delight in the Lord" can mean something a little different for each of us. For some it means communing with Him in prayer. For others, it is the joy of embracing a community that pushes its members to be closer to their faith. For others still, it involves including God in personal areas of life and seeing Him in art, nature, and the smaller things. When God becomes the source of our delight, our joy becomes constant and never-ending.

12

*"Do not fear, for I am with you; do not be dismayed,
for I am your God. I will strengthen you and help you;
I will uphold you with my righteous right hand."*

Isaiah 41:10

When fear threatens to overwhelm us, God's word to us is clear: "Do not fear." He knows our tendency to be afraid, but He is also certain of His power to calm our anxious hearts. As our loving Father, He reassures us of His constant presence and steadfast love.

Just as a loving parent holds their child securely in their arms, so too does God hold us close to His heart, never willing to let us go.

13

"This is what the Lord Almighty says: 'Return to me.'"

Zechariah 1:3

In a few simple words, Zecharia 1:3 encompasses a profound understanding of our relationship with God. In the end, what He really wants is for every single one of His beloved children to return to Him, truly and completely.

The Lord yearns for the recognition and acceptance of His children, and part of our Christian journey is about ensuring that we are constantly finding our way back to Him. When we are strong and confident in our faith, we can turn to our next mission - to help others around us return to Him, too, discovering the wonders His presence can bring.

14

"In your relationships with one another,
have the same mindset as Christ Jesus: Who, being in
very nature God, did not consider equality with God
something to be used to his own advantage."

Philippians 2:5-6

Jesus possessed all the rights and privileges of deity. Yet, He willingly chose to set aside His godliness and take on the form of a servant for the sake of humanity. He never sought personal gain but humbly committed Himself to His people and made the ultimate sacrifice for them.

In turn, we are called to follow His example in our interactions with others. Instead of seeking to assert our own rights, we must consider the needs and interests of others above our own, putting the well-being of others before our own desires.

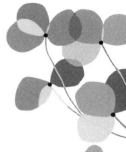

15

"He was with God in the beginning.
Through him all things were made;
without him nothing was made that has been made."

John 1:2-3

John's Gospel begins with a declaration about the eternal nature of Jesus Christ. We learn that Jesus existed with God from the very beginning of time and played a pivotal role in the creation of the universe.

The fact that Jesus was present with God in the beginning emphasizes His eternality. He is not merely a human teacher or religious figure; He is one with He who created the universe and gave us life.

16

"Command them to do good, to be rich in good deeds,
and to be generous and willing to share."

1 Timothy 6:18

Paul emphasizes the importance of two central values in Christian life: doing good deeds and being generous and willing to share in our blessings with others. If we combine these two virtues and successfully embed them in our daily routine so that we do them without even thinking about it, we take a step closer to a life of righteousness and faith.

Let us look for opportunities to bless others, to alleviate suffering, and to lavish upon others what we have so generously been given.

October

17

*"Do not be anxious about anything,
but in every situation, by prayer and petition,
with thanksgiving, present your requests to God."*

Philippians 4:6

Anxiety is a common struggle faced by many, especially in today's fast-paced and uncertain world. It can consume our thoughts, steal our joy, and hinder our progress. However, Paul's words remind us that we do not have to be controlled by anxiety; instead, we can find peace and comfort in prayer.

In cultivating a lifestyle of prayer and gratitude, we experience true peace, guarding our hearts and minds in Christ Jesus.

18

*"But you, Lord, are a compassionate and gracious God,
slow to anger, abounding in love and faithfulness."*

Psalm 86:15

These attributes of our Lord reveal the heart of our Heavenly Father towards His children, offering us comfort, hope, and assurance in His unfailing love. Let us take comfort in the compassionate heart of our God. Let us rest in His grace, knowing that His love for us is unchanging and unconditional. Let us surrender our fears and anxieties to Him, trusting in His faithfulness to carry us through every trial and triumph.

19

"Worship the Lord in the splendor of his holiness;
tremble before him, all the earth."

Psalm 96:9

When we worship God, we are acknowledging His transcendence—that He is separate and distinct from all creation, infinitely pure and righteous in His character. Our worship flows from a deep sense of awe and wonder at who God is and all He has done for us.

To tremble before Him is to recognize our relative insignificance in comparison to His greatness. We do so not only between the walls of a church building, but in every aspect of our lives.

20

"For since the creation of the world God's invisible
qualities — his eternal power and divine nature —
have been clearly seen, being understood from what
has been made, so that people are without excuse."

Romans 1:20

From the grandeur of the highest mountains to the intricate details of a butterfly's wings, every aspect of the natural world testifies to the majesty, power, and wisdom of our Creator.

Yet, despite the clear revelation of God's existence and attributes in creation, humanity often fails to acknowledge Him. Therefore, we, His children, are called to reflect on the revelation of God in creation and respond with awe, reverence, and gratitude for all to see and hear.

October

21

"That is why a man leaves his father and mother and is united to his wife, and they become one flesh."

Genesis 2:24

The union of marriage is so precious to God that it mirrors the unity of Christ and His Church. When two individuals choose to leave their respective families and unite in a bond built on love, commitment, and generosity, their union is blessed and encouraged by the Lord.

He gives them the tools they need to successfully navigate the hurdles of a long-term relationship and the strength they need to turn their home and family into a faithful, righteous unit in Christ.

22

"Live such good lives among the pagans that, though they accuse you of doing wrong, they may see your good deeds and glorify God on the day he visits us."

1 Peter 2:12

Peter challenges believers to conduct themselves in such a way that even those who oppose them cannot deny the goodness and righteousness of their actions.

This is a fundamental part of being a good Christian - being an ambassador of His words and deeds and spreading His glory through the world so that it cannot be mistaken.

23

*"The Lord is my strength and my shield;
my heart trusts in him, and he helps me."*

Psalm 28:7

When we place our trust in God, we experience His faithful provision and intervention in our lives. He comes to our aid, offering His guidance, wisdom, and support in times of need. When we surrender our concerns and fears to Him, He responds with His loving care and assistance, helping us navigate life's challenges with confidence and peace.

When we have Him, nothing else can hurt us, at least not in the spiritual sense. For we are secure and safe in His divine protection.

24

*"Do not be afraid of those who kill the body but
cannot kill the soul. Rather, be afraid of the One
who can destroy both soul and body in hell."*

Matthew 10:28

Fear of other people, both familiar and strangers to us, often tempts us to compromise our beliefs, values, and convictions in order to avoid rejection. We may be tempted to prioritize our physical safety and well-being over our spiritual integrity.

But when we choose to fear God above all else, we recognize that our ultimate loyalty belongs to Him alone, and He holds both our present and our future securely.

25

"Love the Lord your God with all your heart and with all your soul and with all your strength."

Deuteronomy 6:5

Have you ever loved something or someone so much you thought you would burst? That is the kind of love that our Heavenly Father has for us, and the love that He deserves from us in return.

To love the Lord with all our heart means prioritizing Him above all else, allowing Him to occupy a central place in our affections and desires. When we love God with all our heart, our soul, and our strength, we hold nothing back but surrender ourselves completely to Him.

26

"Walk in obedience to him, and keep his decrees and commands, his laws and regulations, as written in the Law of Moses. Do this so that you may prosper in all you do and wherever you go."

1 Kings 2:3

King David imparts a crucial principle to his son Solomon: the path to prosperity lies in obedience to God's commands. Obedience to God is about cultivating a heart that is devoted to His purposes and acknowledging God and trusting in His wisdom and guidance for our lives. Our obedience opens the door for God to work in and through us, enabling us to fulfill the plans and purposes He has for us. It is not about earning God's favor through our actions but rather responding to His grace with gratitude and submission.

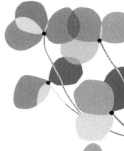

27

*"The Lord God formed the man from the dust of the
ground and breathed into his nostrils the breath of life,
and the man became a living being."*

Genesis 2:7

This passage from Genesis portrays the moment when God
intimately forms the first human being, Adam, from the dust
of the ground, infusing him with the very breath of life.

This act of God breathing life into Adam symbolizes the spiritual
essence and vitality with which God endows humanity. It reminds
us that we are not mere products of chance or evolution but
intentional creations of a loving and purposeful Creator. We are
beautiful, intricate creations made in His image and by His hands.

28

*"We who are strong ought to bear with the failings
of the weak and not to please ourselves."*

Romans 15:1

As followers of Christ, we are called to imitate His example of
selflessness and sacrificial love. Jesus Himself demonstrated
this principle as He tended to the broken, the hurting, and the marginalized. He showed compassion to the weak and weary, offering
them hope, healing, and restoration.

It's important to remember that we all face times when we are
weak and in need of God's grace. None of us are perfect, but by
extending grace and understanding to others, we reciprocate the
love and mercy that God has shown us.

October

29

*"He will cover you with his feathers,
and under his wings you will find refuge."*

Psalm 91:4

The imagery of a bird sheltering its young under its wings accurately illustrates the safety and security that believers can find in God's presence.

God's loving arms provide a place of refuge and safety in the midst of life's storms and struggles. In His presence, we find comfort, peace, and protection from the dangers that surround us.

Let us rest securely in His care, trusting that He will never leave us nor forsake us.

30

*"The Lord is close to the brokenhearted
and saves those who are crushed in spirit."*

Psalm 34:18

Perhaps it has happened to you before that just when you were at your most broken and ready to give up, that is when you suddenly felt your connection with God flare brighter and stronger.

The Lord recognizes when we struggle, he sees our hardships. He knows when we need a helping hand and an encouraging push, and that is when He reveals Himself to us as a friend, mentor, and supporter. Do not be discouraged when things are hard - rather, seek Him even more than you would, because He is there, waiting with open arms.

31

*"The memory of the righteous will be a blessing,
but the name of the wicked will rot."*

Proverbs 10:7

Righteousness has a lasting impact that extends beyond our lifetime and existence. The memory of the righteous is a blessing to those who knew them and to future generations. Their lives serve as examples of faithfulness and love and their legacy continues to inspire and encourage others long after they have passed away.

Remember this whenever you struggle to see the results of your hard work - they reach far into the future and into the souls that surround you.

November

1

*"But seek first his kingdom and his righteousness,
and all these things will be given to you as well."*

Matthew 6:33

Our relationship with God is a mutual, living thing. We cannot expect to simply receive and receive without giving anything in return. And what we are expected to give, what is most valued in God's eyes, is our active search for Him and His closeness. When we seek Him and imbue ourselves in righteousness, we fulfill our end or the covenant and earn the privilege of His many wonderful blessings.

2

"For no word from God will ever fail."

Luke 1:37

The Bible presents countless examples of God fulfilling His promises to His people. God has consistently demonstrated His faithfulness in keeping His word. Every promise He has made is backed by His unfailing faithfulness and sovereignty. When God speaks, His word accomplishes what He desires and achieves the purpose for which He sent it. He is the same yesterday, today, and forever.

3

"For I am convinced that neither death nor life,
neither angels nor demons, neither the present nor the future,
nor any powers, neither height nor depth, nor anything
else in all creation, will be able to separate us from
the love of God that is in Christ Jesus our Lord."

Romans 8:38-39

There is no force on this Earth that is more powerful than that of the love of Christ. No enemy or demon can sever the ties that our Heavenly Father so lovingly extends to us, not now and not ever.

Rest safe and easy in knowing that the love of our Father is something that you will never, ever lose.

4

"And receive from him anything we ask, because
we keep his commands and do what pleases him."

1 John 3:22

In 1 John 3:22, we are given a profound promise: that when we align our lives with God's commands and seek to do what pleases Him, we can confidently receive anything we ask from Him.

The promise of receiving anything we ask from God is not an invitation to fulfill our every whim and desire. Rather, it is a reassurance that if we live a life that is good and faithful to Him, He will grant us the honest and authentic desires of our hearts.

165

5

*"And without faith it is impossible to please God,
because anyone who comes to him must believe that he
exists and that he rewards those who earnestly seek him."*

Hebrews 11:6

Faith involves more than intellectual acknowledgment of God's existence. It requires a deep conviction and trust in His promises and His ability to fulfill them. It is an active, living faith that propels us to rely on God's guidance and provision.

Faith has two key components: believing that God exists, and believing that He rewards those who seek them.

Search your heart and your mind, and consider whether your faith still needs some work.

6

*"I love you, Lord, my strength. The Lord is my rock,
my fortress and my deliverer; my God is my rock,
in whom I take refuge, my shield and the horn
of my salvation, my stronghold."*

Psalm 18:1-2

David in his psalm teaches us an important message about the role that God plays in our lives. Not just an omnipotent God who rules distantly from above, if we embrace Him in our lives and accept him in our hearts He can be so much more for us. He can be our deliverer, who saves us from sin and evil. He can be our fortress and our rock, a place of refuge from the challenges and difficulties of life. And He can be our shield and our salvation, the ultimate friend and father in times of need.

7

*"The Lord is my light and my salvation—whom shall I fear?
The Lord is the stronghold of my life—
of whom shall I be afraid?"*

Psalm 27:1

We often face situations and circumstances that can cause fear and anxiety to rise within us. Whether it's uncertainty about the future, threats to our safety, or challenges that seem insurmountable, fear has a way of gripping our hearts and minds, paralyzing us from moving forward in faith.

However, when we recognize and acknowledge the Lord as our light and salvation, our perspective shifts. We understand that He is the source of our strength, our hope, and our security, and we can let go of the fear that cripples us.

8

*"You will be enriched in every way so that you can be
generous on every occasion, and through us your
generosity will result in thanksgiving to God."*

2 Corinthians 9:11

God desires to cultivate a beautiful circle of mutual generosity and enrichment among His children. Instead of hoarding wealth or resources for ourselves, God calls us to share what we have with others freely. In doing so, we not only meet the needs of those around us but also bask in the joy and fulfillment that come from giving.

November

9

*"Where you go I will go, and where you stay I will stay.
Your people will be my people and your God my God.
Where you die I will die, and there I will be buried."*

Ruth 1:16-:17

Ruth delivers these deeply emotional words to her mother-in-law, Naomi, when she urges her to go on without her. Widowed of her husband and separated from her family, Naomi is all that Ruth has left in the world. But even though they are not related by blood, Ruth's complete devotion to Naomi is an example to us all - to stick with the people we are committed to, and to recognize a good and faithful companion when we see one. Ruth was blessed with a new love, a new family, and renewed faith, thanks to her loyalty to a woman who needed her.

10

*"To the pure, all things are pure, but to those who are
corrupted and do not believe, nothing is pure. In fact,
both their minds and consciences are corrupted."*

Titus 1:15

The purity of your heart is not contained within your heart alone. When you cultivate a pure, loving, and faithful heart, that purity extends beyond just yourself and colors your life, surroundings, and loved ones, too.

Similarly, corruption has a way of seeping through to those around you, as well. Those whose hearts and minds are corrupt and disbelieving cast that same corruption upon their closest circles as well. Let us do all we can to maintain the purity of our hearts, for our own sakes and the sakes of the people we love.

11

*"Two are better than one, because they have
a good return for their labour."*

Ecclesiastes 4:9

Companionship is a natural desire for humans. We crave closeness with others and are naturally drawn to groups and social
gatherings.

Whether it be romantic companionship, friendship, family, or
community, our souls and minds crave human connection.

The Bible emphasizes this beautifully by stating simply that,
"two are better than one." The more the merrier! The more people
we have in our orbit, the more support we have for our spiritual and
emotional journey through life. So embrace those people around
you who are a positive force in your life, and together, the return for
your labor of faith will be so much more significant.

12

*"In their hearts humans plan their course,
but the Lord establishes their steps."*

Proverbs 16:9

A delicate balance exists between our plans and God's divine
guidance. While we may meticulously plan our paths to navigate life's journey according to our own understanding, it is ultimately the Lord who determines our steps.

Imagine a guiding hand, gently steering you left or right, sup-
plementing your limited perspective with endless wisdom.

Find peace in knowing that each day, He is watching
over you and actively involved in directing your steps.

November

13

*"Lord, you have seen this; do not be silent.
Do not be far from me, Lord. Awake, and rise to my defense!
Contend for me, my God and Lord."*

Psalm 35:22-23

In this Psalm, David fervently cries out to the Lord for help and defense against his adversaries. He pleads for God's active involvement, urging Him not to remain silent or distant but to rise up and contend on his behalf.

David demonstrates the openness we can achieve in our relationship with God. When we become truly one with Him, we can approach Him like a friend or a father, pleading with Him when we need His help. In return, He will fight for our cause without reservation.

14

*"So then, just as you received Christ Jesus as Lord,
continue to live in him, rooted and built up in him,
strengthened in the faith as you were taught,
and overflowing with thankfulness."*

Colossians 2:6-7

The Christian journey begins with receiving Christ Jesus as Lord, a moment of surrender and transformation that sets the foundation for a lifetime of growth. However, it doesn't end there.

To be rooted in Christ is all about deepening our relationship with Him, allowing His truth to shape our thoughts, words, and actions. This spiritual growth and maturity happens within the community of believers, where we encourage and support one another in our faith journey.

15

*"And my God will meet all your needs according
to the riches of his glory in Christ Jesus."*

Philippians 4:19

Philippians 4:19 serves as a comforting reminder of God's promise to meet all our needs. It's not just a promise of provision; it's a declaration of abundance, tailored to the unique circumstances of each believer. Our God does not operate within the limitations of human economy.

When we face times of scarcity, we can rest assured that our God is not limited by what we see or understand. Our responsibility, then, is to trust Him wholeheartedly and trust that He will provide.

16

*"They will have no fear of bad news;
their hearts are steadfast, trusting in the Lord."*

Psalm 112:7

When we put our wholehearted trust in the Lord, fear loses its grip on us. We no longer need to be consumed by anxiety over what the future may hold or by the barrage of negative reports around us. Instead, we can face each day with courage and resilience, knowing that our God is with us every step of the way.

And even when bad news does inevitably come, we have a strong foundation of faith built in advance to shield and protect us and help us weather whatever storm is coming.

17

"I tell you, my friends, do not be afraid of those
who kill the body and after that can do no more."

Luke 12:4

Jesus addresses His disciples, calling them friends, emphasizing the intimacy of His relationship with them. He acknowledges the very real threats they may face, even the threat of death itself. However, He urges them—and us—not to be consumed by fear. Why? Because He offers a far wider perspective.

For we who believe in Christ, death is not the end; it is merely a transition into eternity. Jesus is reminding us that there is something far greater at stake than just our physical lives. Our souls are eternal, and our ultimate destiny is in the hands of our Heavenly Father.

18

"For I am the Lord your God who takes hold of your right
hand and says to you, do not fear; I will help you."

Isaiah 41:13

As kids, when we stumble, our parents or guardians take hold of our hand to steady us, help us across the street or up the stairs, until we are grown enough to look after ourselves.

In the same way, God promises to be watchful by our side, taking our hand in support when we need it. He walks alongside us, allowing us to try and fail, but always there to ensure we can rise up after a fall.

19

*"For now we see only a reflection as in a mirror;
then we shall see face to face. Now I know in part;
then I shall know fully, even as I am fully known."*

1 Corinthians 13:12

In our journey of faith, there are moments when we long for clarity, for a clear understanding of God's plans and purposes. Yet, our understanding is limited, akin to seeing a reflection in a mirror. We grasp only fragments of God's infinity, struggling to see beyond our obstructed view.

It's easy to become frustrated by the unanswered questions, but even in our limited understanding, there is beauty. Our partial comprehension of God's ways is a reminder that we are not meant to have all the answers but to trust in He who does.

20

*"Encourage one another daily,
as long as it is called today."*

Hebrews 3:13

Each day is brand new, a fresh start for us all. There is something about resting your head on a pillow, succumbing to dreams, and awakening under a new sun that is restorative to our health, perspective, and mind.

And with each day, come new opportunities. The Bible urges us to see each day as a chance to uplift and support our brothers and sisters in Christ. Whether through a kind word, a listening ear, or a gesture of love, we have the power to make a positive difference in someone's life.

21

"Woe to those who go to great depths to hide their plans from the Lord, who do their work in darkness and think, 'Who sees us? Who will know?'"

Isaiah 29:15

Isaiah delivers a brutally honest truth—no matter how secret or under wraps we feel our actions and emotions are kept, it is naïve to think that they are hidden in any way from our all-knowing Lord. He sees everything, and He knows everything—for good and bad. He is in the deepest crevices of our hearts and minds, seeing the very raw truth of who we are and what we want. There is no point in trying to hide from him—instead, embrace the fact that He is in every aspect of your being, and lean into that beautiful, wonderful companionship.

22

"And what does the Lord require of you? To act justly and to love mercy and to walk humbly with your God."

Micah 6:8

Despite how it may seem, the Lord requires very little of us. In fact, He gives far more than He demands. Everything we have is from Him—our health, our family, our friends, our intelligence, even our belongings. And in return? All he asks of us is for three simple things: to act justly, love mercy, and walk humbly with Him.

Acting justly is employing that same intelligence and judgment he has blessed us with to tell right from wrong. To love mercy is simply to behave with kindness and forgiveness toward others. And humility is knowing and accepting that we are but one small part of a vast, complicated world He has built.

23

"When you pass through the waters, I will be with you; and when you pass through the rivers, they will not sweep over you. When you walk through the fire, you will not be burned; the flames will not set you ablaze."

Isaiah 43:2

The Bible in Isaiah compares the struggles of everyday life with rough waters, sweeping rivers, and blazing fires. Sometimes, it can seem that way—we feel swept along, out of control, or ablaze with anger or fear.

But the true believer knows that however scary or debilitating these trials may be, they will never vanquish us. God protects us every step of the way, looking out for his Children as a father does. Do not be discouraged—instead, trust in Him and know you will be stronger.

November

24

*"He humbled you, causing you to hunger and
then feeding you with manna, which neither you
nor your ancestors had known, to teach you that
man does not live on bread alone but on every word
that comes from the mouth of the Lord."*

Deuteronomy 8:3

The manna that God granted the Israelites as they wandered the desert in search of a land of their own is a symbol to us, even today.

In lieu of meat and bread, the manna was a tasteless substance, a form of nourishment bequeathed lovingly by God in a barren place.

Just as the Israelites did not need bread or material things to endure, so can we be satisfied with things that are beyond the physical world—relying on the wondrous Word of God to sustain us in every way that matters.

25

*"For the foolishness of God is wiser than human wisdom,
and the weakness of God is stronger than human strength."*

1 Corinthians 1:25

Sometimes, we forget just how great God really is. He is the epitome of all that is powerful, kind, and good. He is stronger than the strongest of men, wiser than the wisest of women, purer than the purest of babies.

His sheer greatness must shine a light on our life, humbling us and showing us a path of faith and commitment to our Heavenly Father.

26

"Administer true justice; show mercy and compassion to one another. Do not oppress the widow or the fatherless, the foreigner or the poor. Do not plot evil against each other."

Zechariah 7:9-10

We live in a world where we are surrounded at all times by people both more and less fortunate than us. There will always be someone with more money, more fame, and more freedom. But just the same, we must not forget about those of us with less. Those who come from harsher circumstances, whom life has dealt a less generous hand.

These men, women, and children are our responsibility and we should look out for them and do what we can to help them—applying God's wish that we show mercy and compassion to one another.

27

"Therefore, since we have been justified through faith, we have peace with God through our Lord Jesus Christ."

Romans 5:1

Justification, the act of being declared righteous before God, is not something we can achieve through our own efforts, but rather it is a gift bestowed upon us through faith in Christ.

This peace with God is not merely the absence of conflict; it is a deep sense of reconciliation and harmony with our Heavenly Father. Through Jesus Christ, the barrier of sin that once separated us from God has been removed, and we are now able to enjoy unhindered fellowship with Him.

28

*"Praise be to the God and Father of our Lord Jesus Christ,
the Father of compassion and the God of all comfort,
who comforts us in all our troubles,
so that we can comfort those in any trouble
with the comfort we ourselves receive from God."*

2 Corinthians 1:3-4

God is described as the Father of compassion and the God of all comfort. He doesn't promise a life free from hardship, but He does promise to walk with us through every trial and tribulation. He understands our pain and sorrow intimately, and He stands ready to provide the comfort and strength we need to endure.

Yet, God's comfort doesn't end with us. We are called to channel His love and compassion to others, extending that same comfort to those around us who are hurting and in distress.

29

*"A kindhearted woman gains honor,
but ruthless men gain only wealth."*

Proverbs 11:16

There are few things more precious in the life than being truly honored and respected by others. In Proverbs, the Scripture tells us that the key to honor is simple—being kind-hearted. You do not have to be powerful, wealthy, or highly intelligent to be honored. All you need to do is live your life doing good by others and allowing your heart to bask in kindness.

30

*"Do not let any unwholesome talk
come out of your mouths, but only what is helpful
for building others up according to their needs,
that it may benefit those who listen."*

Ephesians 4:29

There is a saying that goes, "If you do not have anything nice to say, don't say anything at all." This important lesson is reinforced in Ephesians 4, when we are urged to allow only helpful and encouraging words to leave our lips.

Our words have the power to hurt or to heal, let us use them only for good, kind, and faithful things.

December

1

*"And be found in him, not having a righteousness
of my own that comes from the law, but that which
is through faith in Christ—the righteousness
that comes from God on the basis of faith."*

Philippians 3:9

In our human nature, we are flawed and incapable of attaining righteousness on our own merit. Thought they are important, no amount of good works or adherence to religious laws alone can earn us favor with God. However, through unquestioning faith in Christ, we become worthy of His righteousness, which is gifted to us freely and lovingly.

2

*"For prophecy never had its origin in the will of man,
but men spoke from God as they were
carried along by the Holy Spirit."*

2 Peter 1:21

Prophecy is one of God's ways of relaying his wishes and commands to his people through human mouths. Not everyone is able or willing to communicate directly with God, so He sends us prophets to speak His words plainly.

But these prophets, though to us they may seem powerful or even god-like, are no more gods than you or I. They are simply blessed with God's will and carried by the holy spirit, acting as vessels of God's desire.

3

*"The world and its desires pass away,
but whoever does the will of God lives forever."*

1 John 2:17

The Bible talks often about the concept of immortality. God, of course, is immortal—He has been here since before the beginning of time and will remain forever. We are no more than mortals—living a short, meaningful life and then passing on to Heaven.

But is there perhaps some part of us that is immortal? This passage tells us that if we do the will of God—we will live forever. Our legacy, our soul, and our commitment to His commands remain long after our bodies have returned to their maker.

4

*"And the peace of God, which transcends
all understanding, will guard your hearts and
your minds in Christ Jesus."*

Philippians 4:7

The peace we gain from walking with God is one that transcends human comprehension and understanding. It's a peace that isn't dependent on our circumstances but is rooted in our relationship with Christ.

It's a peace that guards our hearts and minds, shielding us from anxiety, fear, and doubt.

God hands us the gift of peace, and all we must do is reach out and accept it.

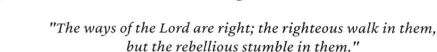

5

"The ways of the Lord are right; the righteous walk in them, but the rebellious stumble in them."

Hosea 14:9

From birth, we encounter two contrasting paths to walk down: the path of the righteous, and the path of the rebellious.

As children, we are guided by our parents. As adults, it is our responsibility to check our steps and ensure that we continue to walk the path of righteousness. This path offers connection, inner strength, and peace, while the other gives nothing more than an uneven road to stumble upon.

6

"In you, Lord, I have taken refuge; let me never be put to shame; deliver me in your righteousness.
Turn your ear to me, come quickly to my rescue;
be my rock of refuge, a strong fortress to save me."

Psalm 31:1-2

Psalm 31:1-2 beautifully expresses the psalmist's trust and dependence on the Lord as their refuge and stronghold.

Like the psalmist, we too can find refuge in the Lord amidst life's trials and challenges. In times of distress, we can turn to Him with confidence, knowing that He is our rock and fortress, our ever-present help in times of trouble, His ear always turned to hear our cries.

7

*"I will lie down and sleep in peace, for you alone,
O Lord, make me dwell in safety."*

Psalm 4:8

Just as children are able to sleep peacefully in their beds, knowing that their parents are there to keep them safe and sound, so can we dwell in safety in our lives, knowing our loving Father watches over us every minute.

None of us are free of anxiety at some time or other. But even in our most stressful times, we can lay back and take a deep breath, finding comfort in the knowledge that we are not alone.

8

*"Don't let anyone look down on you because you are young,
but set an example for the believers in speech,
in conduct, in love, in faith and in purity."*

1 Timothy 4:12

Young or inexperienced people often face feelings of inadequacy or being overlooked because of their age. However, God does not measure our value by our years, but by our obedience and commitment to Him. However young or new to faith you may be, you can set a positive example for others to follow and make Him proud of you.

9

"Charm is deceptive, and beauty is fleeting;
but a woman who fears the Lord is to be praised."

Proverbs 31:30

Our world puts great stock in external beauty. From a young age, we are inundated with messages of physical attraction and material looks.

But we know clearly that beauty cannot last. Our bodies change and grow, and it is impossible to hold to the standard of beauty that society expects of us women.

But our Lord cares not at all how we look on the outside—only who we are on the inside. In the same way that you care for your looks, make sure not to neglect your true self, working on what truly counts: reverence, kindness, compassion, integrity, and humility.

10

"In the same way, let your light shine before others,
that they may see your good deeds and
glorify your Father in heaven."

Matthew 5:16

As followers of Jesus, we are called to live lives that reflect His character and teachings. This means demonstrating kindness, compassion, humility, and integrity in all that we do. When we live in obedience to God's Word and exhibit good deeds, our actions speak volumes about our faith and the God we serve. When we shine with the light of Christ, others are drawn to Him, and we are blessed to be able to live out our faith in real, tangible ways.

11

"First seek the counsel of the Lord."

1 Kings 22:5

You are blessed to have many people in your life whom you can go to for counsel. Perhaps you have a strong relationship with a parent, a significant other who gives excellent advice, or a friend who is always there for you. It is important to have a network of support around you for difficult times, but you must also remember that the Lord is always there to provide counsel in a struggle.

You can go to Him for answers, for advice, even just for a sympathetic ear. He will be there for you, waiting to hear your troubles and to help you through to better days.

12

"It teaches us to say "No" to ungodliness and worldly passions, and to live self-controlled, upright and godly lives in this present age, while we wait for the blessed hope—the appearing of the glory of our great God and Savior, Jesus Christ."

Titus 2:12-13

We believers are called to be distinct from the culture around us. We are called to firmly say "no" to anything that leads us away from God's will and purpose for our lives. Instead, we are expected to pursue righteousness, following the example set by Jesus Christ.

While we strive to live godly lives in the present age, we do so with the anticipation of Christ's return. This hope sustains us, motivates us, and shapes our priorities as we eagerly await the fulfillment of God's promises.

13

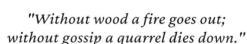

"Without wood a fire goes out;
without gossip a quarrel dies down."

Proverbs 26:20

Just as a fire will die out quickly if it cannot sustain itself with wood, arguments and grudges cannot persist without the fuel of gossip. Idle words and rumors have such incredible negative power to fuel conflict, and frankly, do not have a single redeeming quality.

To engage in gossip is to knowingly fan the flames of discord. Instead, let us strive always to be peacemakers among our fellow believers. Let us encourage honesty, humility, and reconciliation and be a beacon of hope and fairness to our surroundings.

14

"Wine is a mocker and beer a brawler;
whoever is led astray by them is not wise."

Proverbs 20:1

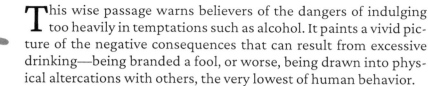

This wise passage warns believers of the dangers of indulging too heavily in temptations such as alcohol. It paints a vivid picture of the negative consequences that can result from excessive drinking—being branded a fool, or worse, being drawn into physical altercations with others, the very lowest of human behavior.

While moderate drinking is not inherently sinful, and indeed, wine plays a large part in our beloved Christian traditions, the potential for abuse and harm is real. Therefore, it's essential to approach alcohol with caution and discernment, knowing the risks involved.

15

"But if we walk in the light, as he is in the light,
we have fellowship with one another, and the blood of Jesus,
his Son, purifies us from all sin."

1 John 1:7

The Bible presents us with a wholesome invitation: to walk in the light, just as God Himself does.

Walking in the light means committing our lives to the truth of God's Word and His character. It involves living in obedience to His commands and allowing His truth to illuminate every corner of our hearts and minds. When we walk in the light, we are rewarded with deep fellowship with God and with our fellow believers, and redemption from all our sins.

16

"For God so loved the world that he gave his one
and only Son, that whoever believes in him
shall not perish but have eternal life."

John 3:16

Christ, our Lord and Savior, was given to us as a gift from a loving God. Imagine the sacrifice of giving up one's child for the sake of the greater good, and you will begin to understand just what a blessing has been bestowed upon us as children of God.

We must cherish this gift and protect it, believing in Him with all our hearts and thus discovering the key to eternal spiritual existence.

17

"Make every effort to add to your faith goodness;
and to goodness, knowledge; and to knowledge,
self-control; and to self-control, perseverance;
and to perseverance, godliness; and to godliness,
mutual affection; and to mutual affection, love."

2 Peter 1:5-7

2 Peter presents us with a step-by-step map to spiritual growth—a progression of virtues that build upon one another to form a mature and Christ-like character. Each virtue listed in this passage represents a vital aspect of Christian character and discipleship. Together, they form a strong base for spiritual work, guiding us toward a deeper relationship with God and a more fruitful life of service to others.

18

"Do not judge, and you will not be judged.
Do not condemn, and you will not be condemned.
Forgive, and you will be forgiven."

Luke 6:37

What goes around comes around. In the same way, when we refrain from judging others, from engaging in gossip and condemnation, we protect ourselves from these evils as well.

You can never know what someone else is going through. You don't know what challenges and trials they have faced, the circumstances they come from, or the mental health issues they are battling. So take care to be kind always and to everyone, and to keep from judging others as you would hope not to be judged yourself.

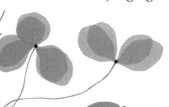

19

*"When Christ, who is your life, appears,
then you also will appear with him in glory."*

Colossians 3:4

As we journey through life, it's easy to become distracted by the temporary concerns and challenges of this world. However, Colossians 3:4 calls us to fix our eyes on an eternal truth. Our lives are not defined by the fleeting circumstances of this world—but by the promise of eternal fellowship with our Savior.

We are challenged to align our priorities, our values, and our pursuits with God. As you await Him, live each day with purpose and devotion.

20

*"Give to everyone what you owe them:
If you owe taxes, pay taxes; if revenue, then revenue;
if respect, then respect; if honor, then honor."*

Romans 13:7

As followers of Christ, we are called to be people of integrity, honoring our commitments and obligations to others. This includes paying taxes and debts promptly, showing respect to authority figures, and giving honor where it is due.

While these may seem like mundane tasks, they reflect our character and witness as believers. By fulfilling our obligations with diligence and integrity, we demonstrate our obedience to God's Word and our commitment to living as His ambassadors in the world.

December

21

*"Sing to the Lord, all the earth;
proclaim his salvation day after day."*

1 Chronicles 16:23

Christian faith is all about praising God's name and singing His virtues. That is why prayer and hymns are such a big part of our lives and traditions. Each occasion on the Christian calendar has its own special songs, and devotions meant to remind us of our duty to proclaim the Word of God to the world.

So sing his praise with pride in your heart and don't be afraid to be vocal about your love for God!

22

*"If we are thrown into the blazing furnace,
the God we serve is able to deliver us from it,
and he will deliver us from Your Majesty's hand."*

Daniel 3:17

When you find yourself in the midst of a personal crisis, battling doubts and fears, or navigating uncertain times, Daniel 3:17 reminds us that our hope rests not in our own strength or abilities, but in the power of our God.

He is a source of strength and encouragement, a light guiding us to safety. May we experience the peaceful assurance that He is always with us, guiding us through the fires of life with His steadfast love and unfailing grace.

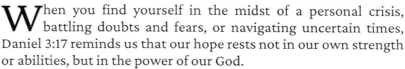

23

"And he has given us this command:
Anyone who loves God must also love
their brother and sister."

1 John 4:21

In just a few words, John encapsulates a profound truth that lies at the very core of Christian faith: the inseparable connection between loving God and loving others. Jesus has given us a fundamental commandment—to love one another as He has loved us.

Loving others isn't easy. It requires humility, forgiveness, and selflessness. It means extending grace and compassion, even to those who may seem undeserving. Yet, it's precisely through our love for others that the world witnesses the transformative power of the gospel.

24

"But he said to me, 'My grace is sufficient for you,
for my power is made perfect in weakness.'
Therefore I will boast all the more gladly about my
weaknesses, so that Christ's power may rest on me."

2 Corinthians 12:9

This verse is a powerful declaration of God's sufficiency in our lives, especially in times of weakness. God's grace is more than enough to sustain us through every trial and challenge we face. In our moments of vulnerability and inadequacy, God's power is made perfect. Our weaknesses are not a source of shame or discouragement—they are an opportunity for Christ's power to be revealed in us.

December

25

"Man is like a breath;
his days are like a fleeting shadow."

Psalm 144:4

Life is short—like a passing breath or a fleeting shadow, our days on earth go by quickly. That is why it is so important to live with purpose and intentionality, while making the most of each moment, cherishing the time we have, and investing it wisely.

The Bible encourages us to prioritize what truly matters. Loving God, ourselves, our families, and our loved ones, and living in faith. Do not be discouraged by the thought that your days are numbered—instead, see it as an opportunity to live each second with meaning.

26

"The fear of the Lord is the beginning of wisdom,
and knowledge of the Holy One is understanding."

Proverbs 9:10

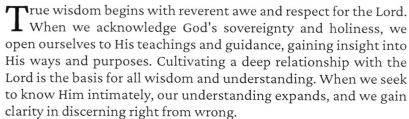

True wisdom begins with reverent awe and respect for the Lord. When we acknowledge God's sovereignty and holiness, we open ourselves to His teachings and guidance, gaining insight into His ways and purposes. Cultivating a deep relationship with the Lord is the basis for all wisdom and understanding. When we seek to know Him intimately, our understanding expands, and we gain clarity in discerning right from wrong.

27

"Glory in his holy name;
let the hearts of those who seek the Lord rejoice."

1 Chronicles 16:10

As we go about the banalities of daily life, we should remember these wise words from the Old Testament, particularly what they imply: that we must actively *seek* the Lord, search for Him in all that we think and do, and only then can we rejoice in His name.

It is our responsibility as God's beloved children to ingrain our faith and its practical applications into every hour of every day, seeking Him always and rejoicing at times where He is found.

28

"Do not let my heart be drawn to what is evil
so that I take part in wicked deeds along with those
who are evildoers; do not let me eat their delicacies."

Psalm 141:4

Evil has a way of drawing us to it. It can often seem shiny and tempting, drawing us away from the path of good and onto a trail we do not truly want to walk.

So, we ask God to give us strength to resist the elusive delicacies and temptations of the evildoers that surround us, guiding us instead gently in the direction of kindness, faith, and good.

December

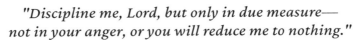

29

"Discipline me, Lord, but only in due measure—
not in your anger, or you will reduce me to nothing."

Jeremiah 10:24

J eremiah pleads with the Lord for discipline tempered with mercy. He acknowledges the necessity of correction but implores God to administer it with kindness and compassion, rather than in anger. In addition to teaching us much about God's method of ruling with kindness, we can learn a lot about enforcing discipline in our own lives—whether in our family, workplace, or even with ourselves, we must remember always to be compassionate, even when scolding or correcting.

30

"Once you were not a people, but now you are
the people of God; once you had not received mercy,
but now you have received mercy."

1 Peter 2:10

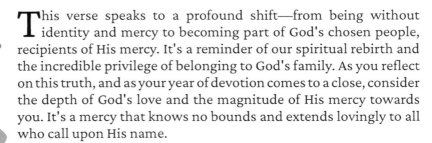

T his verse speaks to a profound shift—from being without identity and mercy to becoming part of God's chosen people, recipients of His mercy. It's a reminder of our spiritual rebirth and the incredible privilege of belonging to God's family. As you reflect on this truth, and as your year of devotion comes to a close, consider the depth of God's love and the magnitude of His mercy towards you. It's a mercy that knows no bounds and extends lovingly to all who call upon His name.

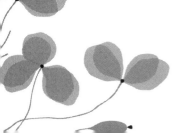

31

*"Keep this Book of the Law always on your lips;
meditate on it day and night, so that you may be
careful to do everything written in it.
Then you will be prosperous and successful."*

Joshua 1:8

Making time for daily devotions is like nourishing our souls with God-given love and truth. It's an opportunity to deepen our understanding of God's character, His promises, and His will for our lives, as well as improve our connection with Him and with ourselves. When we devote ourselves to studying and meditating on God's Word, we align our hearts and minds with His purposes, leading to spiritual growth and obedience.

I hope this year of devotion has lifted your soul and brought you to a better, happier place—both spiritually and mentally. Even though you've reached the last devotion in this book, I urge you to continue making time for yourself to be with God and His Word every single day!

Thank you so much for reading
Daily Devotional for Women!

It means the world to us to be able to bring women
just like you everywhere closer to their faith.

I hope you enjoyed your journey
and feel enlightened and blessed.

We'd appreciate it so much if you would consider
going to Amazon and leaving a review.

Your reviews help us bring you more beautiful
and meaningful content like this book.

About Made Easy Press

At Made Easy Press, our goal is to bring you beautifully designed, thoughtful gifts and products.

We strive to make complicated things – easy. Whether it's learning new skills or putting memories into words, our books are led by values of family, creativity, and self-care and we take joy in creating authentic experiences that make people truly happy.

Look out for other books by Made Easy Press here!

Made in United States
Orlando, FL
13 December 2024

55231093R00109